PEZ®

Shawn Peterson

©2007 Krause Publications

Published by

kp **krause publications**
An Imprint of F+W Publications

700 East State Street • Iola, WI 54990-0001
715-445-2214 • 888-457-2873
www.krausebooks.com

Our toll-free number to place an order or obtain
a free catalog is (800) 258-0929.

Library of Congress Catalog Number: 2006934239

ISBN: 978-0-89689-466-2

Designed by David Jensen
Edited by Karen O'Brien

Printed in China

Contents

Editor's Note: All photos are from the author's personal collection and were taken by Steve Warner, except where noted. Some dispensers are listed together in groups and may not follow the alphabetical organization of this book, so check the index for the dispenser in question.

Introduction

Looking back, I think 2006 will be regarded as one of the most important years in PEZ® history. A few key dates really stand out—in 1949 the first PEZ® Box was introduced, and in 1952 PEZ® debuted in America, followed closely by the addition of character heads to the dispenser. In 1987, the addition of feet to the dispenser base was the first noticeable change in many years. Now, almost 20 years later, we are witnessing one of largest changes ever made by the company. The long-standing rule of not putting a real person atop a PEZ® dispenser has been broken, and this could be the most significant change to date, as it opens up possibilities as varied as the people who could be included.

In the fall of 2006, the company will release a tin gift box set featuring the Teutul's, the motorcycle building family featured on the popular Discovery Channel television show, American Chopper. The release of this set will bring a whole new awareness to PEZ® and should create an even wider fan base for this iconic candy. There is also talk of including famous people such as the Beatles and Elvis. This may be the start for a whole new generation of collectors.

PEZ® is also undergoing a corporate transformation that began with the 2004 arrival of a new president, and communication with collectors has increased dramatically. The new president has made it a point to talk with collectors and find out what is on their minds. One of the most visible changes is the increased number of new characters released and sold at your favorite store. PEZ® has become very timely, licensing the hottest characters and coordinating the dispenser release along with the movie—a practice unheard of just a few years ago. The day may not be far away when tours of the PEZ® factory may be offered, or a retail store selling everything PEZ® is open to the public.

PEZ® candy will mark its 80th anniversary in 2007. It will also be the year PEZ® introduces a new mint marketed to adult consumers. These new containers will look similar to a traditional dispenser and will feature selected artwork from two famous artists. The European distribution will have works from Andy Warhol while the domestic version will feature Norman Rockwell. PEZ® is trying to expand its traditional boundaries and tap into new markets.

I feel like I say the same thing every year—this is the most exciting time to collect PEZ®. But PEZ® seems to top themselves every year and come up with something a little more exciting or different that what has been done before. These next couple of years will be no exception. There are some really exciting projects in the works and many new characters on the way. I hope as you look through this guide and enjoy the new additions it will create that spark of passion to collect and enjoy each and every dispenser.

For now, sit back, relax and enjoy nearly 80 years of candy dispensing memories!

Shawn Peterson

PEZ® History

The PEZ® dispenser has been around for just over 50 years. PEZ® candy got its start even earlier, introduced in 1927 in Vienna, Austria, as the world's first-ever breath mint. Edward Haas, an avid non-smoker, wanted to invent a product to rival cigarettes. His product, a small compressed sugar tablet with peppermint oil added, was sold in small pocket size tins (similar to Altoid brand mints of today) and marketed as an alternative to smoking. His slogan was "smoking prohibited-pezzing allowed!" But what is "pezzing," or better yet, PEZ®? The name "Pez" was derived from the German word for peppermint, "pfefferminz." Using the first, middle, and last letter of the word, Haas came up with the name "Pez." Twenty years after the candy was invented, in 1948, Oscar Uxa invented and patented a little mechanical box for dispensing the candy. Resembling a Bic cigarette lighter, the dispenser was marketed as an upscale adult product. The PEZ® "box" had moderate success in Europe, and in 1952 Haas decided to try and conquer the U.S. market. In the span of less than 2 years, he realized that PEZ® was not going to be a worthwhile venture in the United States.

Haas did not give up however, and he decided to reinvent the product by adding fruit flavors to the candy—and a three-dimensional cartoon head to the top of the dispenser. What a success this turned out to be, combining two of kids' favorite things: candy and a toy! This marketing shift proved to be a brilliant move, making PEZ® one of the most recognizable commercial names around. It is hard to say how many different heads have graced the top of a PEZ® dispenser. Different versions of the same character have been produced and, in some cases, the same version has come in multiple color variations. Conservative estimates put the number between 400-450 different heads.

Despite numerous requests for Elvis and others, PEZ® has never depicted a real person with the exceptions of Betsy Ross, Paul Revere, and Daniel Boone. They have followed this policy for two main reasons: real people rarely have interestingly shaped heads, and the possibility of a real person winding up in a front-page controversy makes the thought less than appealing for a children's product. The company also tries to stay away from passing fads, using only characters that have stood the test of time. At any given time, there are as many as 60-70 different dispensers available at local retailers, not to mention the seasonal ones that appear for such holidays as Christmas, Easter, Halloween, and Valentines Day. PEZ® began offering limited edition dispensers in 1998 with remakes of the classic Psychedelic

Hand and Psychedelic Flower. Offered only through the PEZ® Candy Inc. Web site or via phone orders, these limited editions have proven quite popular with collectors.

PEZ®, the company, is divided into two separate entities, PEZ® USA and PEZ® International. PEZ® USA, located in Orange, Connecticut, is responsible for North American distribution, packaging dispensers, and making candy. PEZ® International, now located in Traun, Austria, handles distribution for the rest of the world, along with packaging dispensers and making candy. Although they are separately managed companies, they communicate with each other and sometimes share the cost of producing a new dispenser. The fact that they are two separate companies, and agreements in licensing, account for the reason some dispensers commonly found in the United States are not found anywhere else in the world and vise versa. Depending on how you look at it, this can make collecting more fun or more of a challenge. PEZ® USA is a privately owned business and will not release sales figures to the public, but they do insist that they sell more dispensers per year than there are kids in the United States. Their staff works in three shifts, 24 hours a day, producing the candy and packaging dispensers for shipment all across North America.

The dispenser itself has seen a few modest changes over the years. One of the biggest changes happened in the late 1980s, when "feet" where added to the bottom of the dispenser base to give it more stability when standing upright. Numerous candy and fruit flavors have been produced, ranging from apple to chocolate. Some flavors were more popular than others, and some were just plain strange like chlorophyll, flower, and eucalyptus. Currently the flavors available in the United States are lemon, orange, grape, strawberry, Cola, sour blue raspberry, sour watermelon, sour pineapple, sour green apple, and peppermint.

Although PEZ® has a long history, only recently has it become a hot collectible. PEZ® collecting has been gathering steam since the early 1990s when the first guidebook appeared, depicting all known dispensers and their rarity. The first ever PEZ® convention was held in Mentor, Ohio, on Saturday, June 15, 1991. Several other conventions around the country soon followed. Collectors finally had a chance to meet each other, buy and sell PEZ®, and view rare and unusual dispensers on display. Conventions have quickly become must-attend events for addicted collectors, drawing people from all over the United States and even all over the world.

In 1993, the prestigious Christie's auction house in New York took notice of this evolving hobby and held its first ever pop culture auction featuring

PEZ®. The auction realized record prices, taking the hobby to a new level. PEZ® has been featured in countless magazines, TV shows, and news articles—landing on the cover of Forbes magazine in December of 1993. The popular Seinfeld television show even had an episode featuring a Tweety Bird PEZ® dispenser. All this notoriety hasn't gone unnoticed. More and more people have begun to collect these cute character pieces, sending prices into the hundreds and even thousands of dollars for a single dispenser.

PEZ® has done very little in the way of advertising, relying on impulse purchases and parents buying for their kids on a nostalgic whim. While this may not seem like the best marketing method, the company claims it can barely keep up with demand. PEZ® has even become a very popular licensee, with companies vying to put the PEZ® name on everything from clocks to coffee mugs. Hallmark has featured these collectibles on a puzzle and matching greeting card, and has also produced two different PEZ® dispenser Christmas ornaments.

No one can say for sure where this hobby will go, or if the dispensers will continue to hold their value. In the more than 15 years that I have been a collector, prices, as well as the collector base, have steadily grown. At present, this hobby has two things in its favor: demand far surpasses the supply of vintage dispensers, and PEZ® is still produced today and can be found in almost any grocery or discount store, making it available to a whole new generation of collectors. With new additions added regularly, the continued success of PEZ® is almost certainly assured.

Pricing Information

A price guide should be viewed as just that—a guide. Since this hobby has become organized, PEZ® prices, like the stock market, have been in nearly constant motion. Prices not only go up, but some do go down. Several factors account for this fluctuation: supply and demand, emotion, and quantity finds. To pick a point in time and label a dispenser worth exactly "X" amount of dollars, in my opinion, is not in the best interest of the collector. I feel that an average price system is more useful. I have used several sources—online auctions, dealer's lists, and other collectors—to determine what I feel is an accurate price range for each dispenser. Therefore, a price quoted will not reflect the top or bottom dollar that a dispenser has sold for. Dispensers that do not appear for sale often enough to determine an accurate price range will be represented with a price and the "+" symbol.

This pricing information should be used for dispensers that are complete and void of any missing pieces, cracks, chips, or melt marks, and have working spring mechanisms. Dispensers that are broken or missing pieces are not worth nearly as much as complete dispensers. Pricing incomplete or broken dispensers is very subjective. Missing pieces are almost never found. Some collectors don't mind if a dispenser is broken or missing a piece or two, especially if it is a rare dispenser or variation. They may be happy just to have an example in their collection, and hope to upgrade to a dispenser in better condition.

Generally, the value of a dispenser is in the head. Age, country of origin, stem, and patent numbers can also play a part, but are commonly thought of as non-determining factors when assessing the value. Exceptions to this regarding the stems are features such as die-cuts, advertising, or pictures, such as found on the witch regular. One or more of these features can actually increase the value of the dispenser. Other stem characteristics must be present in certain dispensers to complete the value and be considered correct. For example, the football player stem will have one smooth side with an upside down pennant-shaped triangle molded in. Also, all of the original psychedelics will have at least one, and sometimes two, smooth sides to which a sticker was applied (stickers must still be intact). Swirled or marbleized stems can also add value to a dispenser. Some collectors are willing to pay a bit more for these as they can be very difficult to find and no two are exactly alike. Finally, resale is something you may want to consider. A complete, mint-condition dispenser will always be easier to sell than one that has problems or is missing parts.

A Word of Caution

Collectors beware: Some people have begun making and selling reproduction parts for PEZ®. Some are better skilled at this than others. Trust your instinct. If you think an item is questionable, it is better to pass than find out later that you have been taken. Know what you are buying and be familiar with what a piece should look like.

Some dispensers, such as Elvis and KISS, were never made by PEZ® but can be found with relative ease. How can this be? When a dispenser of a certain character or person is in demand but does not exist, collectors have sometimes resorted to making their own dispensers. These are known as "fan-made" or "fantasy" pieces. Again, some of these pieces are better made than others; in fact, some are quite good. You can even find fantasy pieces that are mint on a very convincing PEZ® card, but in reality never existed. Most of these dispensers sell in the $25 or less range and are considered by some to be very collectable.

Only knowledge, experience, and buying from a well known, reputable dealer will help avoid having a reproduction or fake unknowingly passed on to you. Common reproduction parts include but are not limited to: the ringmaster's moustache, the Mexican's goatee and earrings, the policeman's and fireman's hat badges, the knight's plume, the doctor's reflector, and Batman's cape. Most parts are not labeled as reproductions. For instance, a remake of the doctor's reflector is made of aluminum instead of plastic, and the reproduction capes for Batman are usually much thicker than the vintage capes. Studying pictures in books and going to PEZ® conventions are your best sources for comparing dispensers. A great deal of information can also be found on the Internet. There are many PEZ®-related Web sites made by collectors that will answer almost any question related to the hobby.

How To Use This Book

The dispensers are listed in alphabetical order. The common name of the dispenser is listed first, followed by any alternate names. Next you will find a date—this is when production of the dispenser started. Notes on whether the dispenser was made with or without feet (or both) are also included. Finally, a value will be given for the dispenser as well as for known variations.

Values given are for loose dispensers complete with all working parts, and have no melt marks, cracks, or chips. Pricing packaged dispensers is a bit more subjective. Some collectors have little or no interest in packaged dispensers, as they want to display their collections more creatively. Currently, there is little interest in poly bag packaging. Clear cello bags may add a little value to a dispenser. For example, if the dispenser is worth $50, it might bring $55-$60 if packaged in a clear cello bag. The exceptions to this are dispensers that are packaged with an insert, sticker, comic, advertising, or a rare pack of candy. Sometimes these inserts are worth more than the dispenser. Dispensers mounted on cards are considered the most desirable of packaged dispensers. Factors affecting the value of a carded dispenser are condition of the card, and graphics or artwork on the card. Seasonal cards with neat artwork are worth more than plain, solid-color cards.

Illustrated Glossary

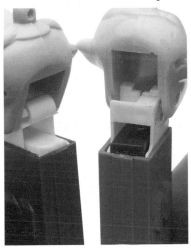

CHANNEL: The groove on the front of the dispenser that runs the length of the stem.

BUTTON: An opaque rectangle piece inside the stem, usually red but sometimes white, that the candy actually sits on. There are a couple versions: a rectangle with square corners, and a rectangle with rounded corners. The square corner version is the oldest.

CLUB MED: A term used when a character's face appears very tan, as if they have been in the sun or at Club Med. This can also be considered a color variation.

COLOR VARIATION: Refers to the comparison of like dispensers in which one has a different color to the entire head or to one or more of the parts found on the head. Example: a cow may have a head that is yellow, blue, orange, green, etc. The possibilities are almost infinite.

DBP: The German patent number on a dispenser. It means "Deutsches Bundes Patent" and will be accompanied by the numbers 818 829.

HEAD: The top-most part of the dispenser that tilts back to dispense the candy.

FEET: Small rounded plastic protrusions or tabs at the base of the stem to help the dispenser stand upright. Feet were added to dispensers in the U.S. around 1987. Currently there are 2 different styles. The earlier version is known as "thin feet," referring to the fact that the plastic of the feet is not as thick as the plastic feet found on current dispensers. Beware, some people try to cut the feet off and pass them off as a footless dispenser. Some dispensers were produced both ways, with feet and without. Look to the spine of the stem to tell if it has been altered.

IMC: Injection Mold Code. A single digit number found on the outside top corner of the stem. Identifies in which plastic factory the dispenser was molded. Not all dispensers have IMC's. Here is a list to help identify which number goes with which country:

1 & 3: Austria/ Hungary
2: Austria/ Hong Kong
4 & 8: Austria
5: Yugoslavia/ Slovenia
6: Hong Kong/ China
7: Hong Kong/ Austria/ Czech Republic
9: U.S.A.
V: Yugoslavia (changed to Slovenia in 1993)

KICKER: Sometimes referred to as the "pusher," this is the small plastic piece that extends down from the back of the head and pushes out a single piece of candy when the head is tilted back.

LOOSE: the dispenser is out of its original packaging.

MARBLEIZED: a term used when two or more colors of plastic are combined and not thoroughly mixed, causing a swirling pattern to appear in the finished product. This is a sought after variation by some collectors.

PATENT NUMBER: Seven-digit number located on the side of the stem. Currently there are five different U.S. patent numbers on PEZ® dispensers: 2,620,061 is the earliest, followed by 3,410,455; 3,845,882; 3,942,683; and 4,966,305. 3,370,746 was issued for the candy shooter and appears on the 1980s space gun as well. Patent numbers can help identify the age of a dispenser, but generally do not play a part in its value. Not all dispensers have a patent number on them, certain dispensers have no patent numbers, and this does not affect the value of those dispensers. Feet first started to appear on dispenser bases when the 3,942,683 number was issued, but some exceptions can be found with feet and earlier issue patent numbers. These dispensers are difficult to find and carry a little more value with some collectors.

MELT MARK: refers to damage on the dispenser. Sometimes caused by direct heat or a chemical reaction between the plastic of the dispenser and certain types of rubber or other plastics. Certain types of rubber bands and items like rubber-fishing worms have been known to cause melt marks when left in contact with a dispenser.

M.I.B.: Mint In Bag. Bag will have colored ends and writing as well as the PEZ® logo. Newer style. Also known as a "poly bag."

M.I.C.: Mint In Cellophane or Mint In Cello. Bag will be clear with no writing.

M.O.C.: Mint On Card.

M.O.M.C.: Mint On Mint Card. Both dispenser and card are in pristine condition.

N/F: no feet.

PEZHEAD: A term used to describe someone who collects PEZ®!

PIN: Steel pin that hinges the head. Made of metal and found only in older dispensers. The pin runs through the side of the head and the sleeve, attaching it to the dispenser base.

REGULAR: The earliest PEZ® dispensers. These didn't have a character head; instead they had only a thumb grip at the top and were marketed for adults. These were remade in the late 1990s, but with a noticeable difference. Vintage regulars will have a raised thumb grip on the top of the cap. The remakes will have a square cap with no raised grip and the spine will be deeper than the channel.

SHOES: An accessory for your dispenser that fits on the base of the stem. Similar to feet in that its purpose is to give the dispenser more stability when standing upright. Originally made to be used with the Make-a-Face dispenser. Reproduction shoes have been made with a rounded toe in the front, and can be found in at least three colors: black, white, and red. There is also a reproduction glow-in-the-dark version. An original shoe will always be black and have a "B" shape to the end.

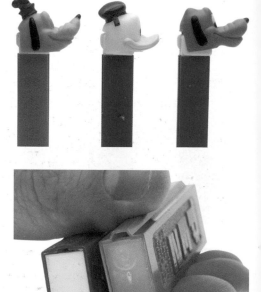

SLEEVE: The part of the dispenser that pulls out of the stem and holds the candy. The United States patent description refers to this part as the magazine.

SOFTHEAD: The head is made of a rubber, eraser-like material that is pliable and softer than traditional plastic head dispensers, hence the name "softhead." Softheads can be found in the Erie Specter and Superhero series, along with a very rare Disney set that never made it to mass production.

SPINE: The groove on the back of the dispenser that runs the length of the stem. On a vintage footless dispenser the spine should be the same depth as the channel. Some unscrupulous people will try to pass off a dispenser as footless by cutting off the feet and claiming that it is old. To detect tampering, turn the dispenser upside down and compare the spine to the channel. The spine on a footed dispenser will always be deeper than its channel.

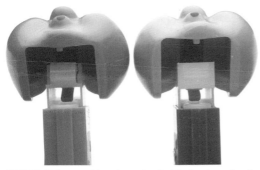

SPRING: Refers to either the spring inside the stem directly under the button, OR the spring in the top of the dispenser that keeps tension on the character head. There are three basic types of springs in the top of the dispenser: the classic wire mechanism, the blade spring, and currently a "leaf spring" mechanism.

STEM: The lower part of the dispenser. Usually has the PEZ® logo on at least one side and possibly country of origin, patent number, and injection mold code. Depending on the dispenser, the stem may also be die-cut or be completely smooth on one or both sides.

TRANSITION PIECE: A dispenser that has characteristics of a previous model, but also has features of a current dispenser. These pieces must still be in their original packaging to show they are void of alterations. Example: an old-style character head that is on a footed stem.

W/F: With feet.

PEZ® Conventions

Do you want to meet other collectors? Have lots of fun? See more PEZ® than you ever imagined? Attend a PEZ® convention! Conventions are one of the best ways to gain information and knowledge of the hobby, as well as to buy and sell PEZ®. You will find many rare and unusual items displayed, as well as organized events such as "Pez Bingo" to keep you busy.

Conventions have been sprouting up since the early 1990s, drawing people from all over the U.S. and the world. Below you will find a current list of conventions, check PEZ Collector's News for exact times and dates.

1.

Southern California – Conventions have been held since 1994 in several different locations with different hosts. Usually meets sometime in the spring.

2.

St. Louis, Missouri – First convention held in 1993 and still going strong. Meets in June. Your host is John "CoolPezman" Devlin, who may be reached using the Web site, http://www.pezconvention.com or the 24-hour hotline: (314) 416-0333.

3.

Bloomington, Minnesota – First convention held in October 1996 across from the Mall of America. Now meets in August rather than October. Your hosts are Dana and Julie Kraft, they may be reached using the Web site, www.MNPEZCON.com

4.

Cleveland, Ohio – First ever PEZ® convention, "Dispensor-O-Rama" held June, 1991 in Mentor, Ohio. Continues to meet each July in the Cleveland area. Your host is Jill Cohen and she may be reached using the Web site, www.pezmania.com or at the following phone number: (216) 283-5993 before 10pm EST.

5.

Connecticut – Called the "East Coast PEZ® Convention" first met in April 1999 in Orange, Connecticut (home of PEZ® Candy, Inc.). Moved to a larger location in Stamford, CT for the May 2000 show. Your host is Richie Belyski (editor of PEZ Collector's News) and he may be reached using the Web site, www.pezcollectorsnews.com or at the following address:

PEZ Collector's News
P.O. Box 14956
Surfside Beach, SC 29587

Finding Information

Several newsletters have been dedicated to collecting PEZ®. The first, The Toy Candy Container and Food Premium Collector, appeared in 1987. With the third issue the name changed to The Old Variety Store. The OVS lasted until late 1989 and had a run of about 15 issues. In January 1990, the Optimistic Pezzimist came on board. It, too, had a run of just 15 issues, lasting until July of 1992. Without much delay, in the fall of 1992 the Positively Pez newsletter was started.

By this time the hobby was gaining steam. The first book about PEZ® had been released during the previous year, and collectors were becoming more knowledgeable than ever. Positively Pez had a run of 19 issues and ended with the January/February 1996 edition. With the announcement of its close, and with an ever-growing number of collectors hungry for the latest PEZ® information, two new publications started. The Fliptop Pezervation Society premiered with the September/October 1995 issue, billing itself as "the first national club for PEZ® collectors." Pedro PEZ®, a boy PEZ® Pal dispenser, was adopted as the club mascot and was sent around the world with various collectors visiting interesting places and having his picture taken.

Right on the heels of the Fliptop newsletter, PEZ® Collector's News made its first appearance with the October/November 1995 issue. The two newsletters worked well together, uniting collectors and giving them more information than ever before. In December 1999, the Fliptop Pezervation Society announced that the September/October 1999 issue was their last and they would combine efforts with PEZ® Collector's News. FPS enjoyed a run of 24 issues. Currently, PEZ Collector's News, put out bimonthly by Richie Belyski, is the only newsletter devoted to PEZ®. You can contact them at:

PEZ Collector's News
P.O. Box 14956
Surfside Beach, SC 29587
E-mail: info@pezcollectorsnews.com
www.pezcollectorsnews.com

PEZ® in Space

PEZ® in Space? Cyberspace, that is. A ton of information about PEZ® can be found on the Internet. It is an excellent source for up-to-date information and a great way to buy and sell PEZ®. There are hundreds, maybe even thousands, of sites built by collectors that detail everything from how to properly load your dispenser to pictures of personal collections.

One of the nicest collector-built sites is Pez Central. Good design, great graphics and pictures, up-to-date information, and links to other Web pages make it a great place to visit. Check it out at: www.pezcentral.com.

By now there are probably very few people who haven't heard of eBay. But did you know that eBay got its start with PEZ®? Pierre Omidyar, founder of eBay, originally created the site as a way for his girlfriend to buy and sell PEZ® dispensers. To accomplish this, Omidyar built an Internet auction site that brought buyer and seller together on a level playing field. In doing so he created one of the most popular and fastest growing places on the Internet. There are now three PEZ® categories—General, Current, and Vintage—which offer an average of more than 3,000 items a week. You can find the site at: www.ebay.com.

PEZ® Candy, Inc. also has a Web site. Within their site you will find a FAQ list (Frequently Asked Questions), a list of PEZ® dispensers offered to date in the United States, a list of other cool PEZ® products, information about PEZ® newsletters, and the PEZ® Store. The store sells many current dispensers and candy flavors, including some items that are unique and only available through the special mail-order program. The site can be found at: www.pez.com.

Starting Up

If you are a new collector, you are probably wondering how to get started. Start out slowly—look for all of the current release dispensers you can find around your town. That alone will give you a nice size collection on which to build without spending too much money. Most collectors ask the questions: "Should I leave it in the package or open it up?" and "Will it loose its value if I open it?" Opening the dispenser is a matter of preference. If the dispenser is old, I would advise against opening the package. With the new stuff, it's up to you. Personally, I buy at least three of each new release; one in the bag, one on the card to save, and one to open for display. It's true, a carded or bagged dispenser is traditionally worth more than one that is loose, but a dispenser out of package is more fun to display.

Next, move on to the current European dispensers. Most of these can be had for $3 to $4 each. Acquire all of these and the size of your collection will almost double. When it comes to vintage dispensers, decide what your first "price plateau" will be and start from there. For example, there are still a good number of footless dispensers that can be found for $25 or less. Once you buy all of these, move on to the next price level and so on.

Although some of the old dispensers reach into the hundreds and even thousands of dollars, you don't have to spend your life savings to enjoy the hobby. Some collectors specialize and focus on collecting one favorite area such as the Animals or PEZ® Pal series. Others focus on stems by collecting a character that is made in several different countries, or by collecting as many different colors as they can. A good example of this is the Teenage Mutant Ninja Turtles. There are eight different dispensers that come on eight different stem colors, if you were to collect all of the combinations you would have 64 turtles alone in your collection!

The most important thing to remember about collecting PEZ® is that it's a hobby—have fun!

Admiral

Late 1960s-1970s, no feet

A very rare dispenser, this is the only one currently known to exist. The Admiral character has been shown on various PEZ® advertisements such as comics and candy boxes, but none had been found until early 2000.

Value: .... **$8000+**

Admiral. **$8000+**

Alpine Man

Early 1970s, no feet

Produced for the 1972 Munich Olympics, this is a very rare and difficult dispenser to find.

Value: .... **$3000+**

Alpine Man. **$3000**
(From the Maryann Kennedy collection.)

Adult Breath Mints

2006 Europe, 2007 United States

The European version will feature four famous works of art from Andy Warhol. The American version will feature four pieces of artwork from Norman Rockwell.

Value: .... **$1-$2**

Adult Breath Mints. **$1-$2**
(KP Photo)

Angel

Early 1970s, no feet and with feet

Several versions of the Angel have been produced, including one with a small plastic loop on the back of her hair that allows it to be used as an ornament.

No feet: ....$85-$100
With feet:..$50-$65
Unusual blond hair version:..............$90-$125
Ornament: ....$100-$125

Angel, removable eye version. **$125-$150**

Unusual version of Angel with loop.
$100-$125
(From the Johann Patek collection.)

Three versions of the Angel dispenser. (L to R) Yellow hair with feet **$50-$65,** yellow hair without feet **$85-$100,** and a rare blonde version **$90-$125.**

Annie

Early 1980s, no feet
Released to coincide with the release of the movie *Annie*. The movie wasn't a hit and neither was the dispenser, making this one a little tough to find.

Value:................................ **$150-$175**

Annie. **$150-$175**

Arithmetic Dispensers

Early 1960s
Arithmetic Regulars were available as a mail-in premium as well as sold in stores. They can be found in red, blue, green, tan, and yellow.

Blue:.................................$500-$700
Green: ....$600-$800
Red:.................................$700-$900
Tan or yellow: ....$800-$1000

Arithmetic dispenser insert.

Arithmetic dispenser, blue version. **$500-$700**

Asterix

Asterix is a popular European comic. These dispensers have not been released in the U.S. The series was first produced by PEZ® in the mid-1970s and a remake of the original series was released in the late 1990s. The remakes have feet and painted on eyes. The Roman Soldier was not included in the original series.

Asterix
Mid-1970s, no feet and with feet

Original: .... $1500-$2000
Remake: .... $3-$5

Obelix
Mid-1970s, no feet and with feet

Original: .... $1500-$2000
Remake: .... $3-$5

Muselix
Mid-1970s, no feet and with feet

Original: .... $2500-$3000
Remake, called "Getafix"
by PEZ: .... $3-$5

Roman Soldier
Late 1990s, with feet

Value: .... $3-$5

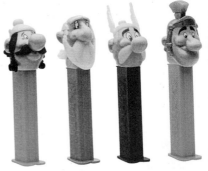

Remake of the Asterix series. (L to R) Obelix, Muselix (sometimes called "Getafix"), Asterix, and Roman Soldier. **$3-$5**

Original Asterix from the mid-1970s. **$1500-$2000**
(From the Maryann Kennedy collection.)

Original Muselix (L) **$2500-$3000** and Obelix (R) **$1500-$2000.**
(Obelix is from the Maryann Kennedy collection.)

Astronaut

Early 1960s, no feet

The Astronaut 1 was not released in the U.S., but the second Astronaut, released in the 1970s was distributed in the U.S. A very rare version of this dispenser exists and is known as the "World's Fair Astronaut" because of the inscription on the left side of the stem. Only two of these dispensers are known to exist—one with a green stem and white helmet and the other with a blue-green stem and matching helmet.

Astronaut 1: .... **$600-$800**
Astronaut 2 white helmet/green stem: ....**$125-$150**
Astronaut 2 blue helmet/blue stem: ....**$140-$160**
World's Fair Astronaut: .... **$8000+**

Astronaut 1, from the early 1960s. This dispenser was not released in the U.S. and can also be found with a white or light blue helmet. **$600-$800**

Astronaut 2 from the late 1970s. White helmet/green stem **$125-$150,** blue helmet/stem **$140-$160.**

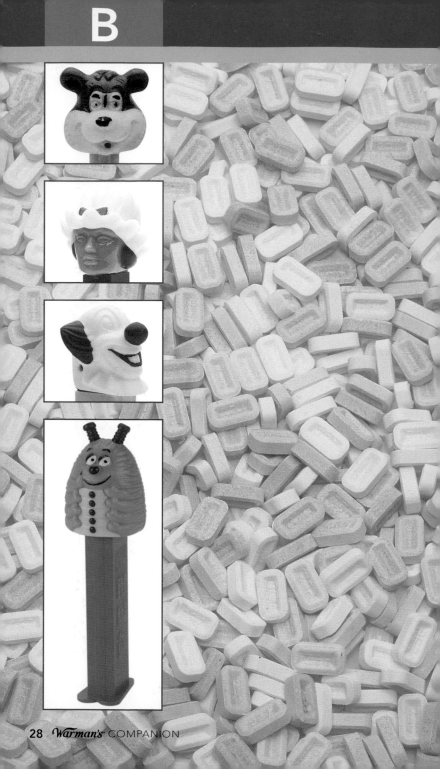

Baloo

Late 1960s, no feet and with feet
Although difficult to find, Baloo was also produced with a yellow or red head.

Blue-gray head, no feet: .... $30-$40
Blue-gray head, with feet: .... $20-$30
Red or Yellow head, no feet: .... $800+

Baloo from the Jungle Book series. **$30-$40**

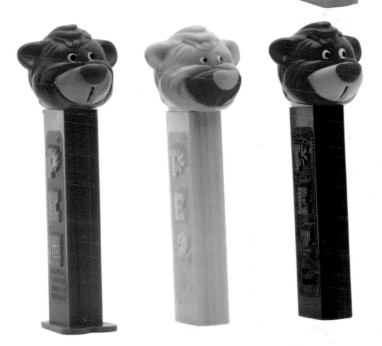

Unusual Baloo variations. **$800+**
(From the Johann Patek collection.)

Bambi

Late 1970s, no feet and with feet
The same mold was used for the Rudolf dispenser but with a black nose. A rare version of this dispenser, although subtle, carries the copyright symbol along with the letters "WDP" on the head, which can at least double the value.

No copyright, no feet: ....$50-$75
No copyright, with feet: ....$35-$45
With copyright, no feet:..............$125-$150

Bambi, from the late 1970s. The same mold was used to make the Rudolph dispenser. **$50-$75**

Barky Brown

2005, with feet

Value:................................$10-$15 each

Barky Brown, loose. **$10-$15**

Barney Bear

Early 1980s, no feet and with feet

No feet: .... $35-$45
With feet: .... $20-$30

Barney Bear, an MGM character released in the early 1980s, yellow stem and feet. **$20-$30**

Barney Bear, with red stem and feet. **$20-$30**

Basketball Pez

2002-2005, with feet
The Seattle Sonics and Washington Mystics women's basketball team dispensers were released in 2002, and the Connecticut Suns dispenser was released in 2005.

Seattle Sonics: ....$30-$40
Washington Mystics: ..$30-$40
Connecticut Suns: ......$25-$30

Seattle Sonics **$30-$40**, Washington Mystics **$30-$40**, and Connecticut Suns **$25-$30**.
(KP Photo)

Baseball Promos
2002-2004, with feet

LSU baseball (2004): ....$25-$35
Philadelphia Phillies (2002): ....$25-$30
Arizona Diamondbacks (2002): ....$25-$35

Baseball promos (L-R): LSU baseball **$25-$35,** Philadelphia Phillies **$25-$30,** Arizona Diamondbacks **$25-$35.**

Baseball Set

Mid-1960s, no feet

This set consisted of a dispenser with a baseball mitt "head" and a removable ball, bat, and home plate. It is difficult to find with the bat and home plate. The vending box is also very rare, as only a few examples are known to have survived. In 2005, a box of 24 mint examples were found with their original vending boxes. Despite this influx, prices have held steady.

Value: ....$600-$800

Baseball set from the mid-1960s with rare vending box. **$600-$800**
(From the Maryann Kennedy collection.)

Backside of rare vending box.
(From the Maryann Kennedy collection.)

Batman

Late 1960s, no feet and with feet

Batman has gone through several different looks and can still be found today. Batman with cape is the earliest version and collectors should be aware that reproductions of the cape have been made. The original cape can be somewhat translucent whereas reproduction capes are much thicker.

Batman with cape: ....$75-$120
Short ears, no feet: ....$20-$30
Short ears, with feet: ....$10-$15
Short ears, with feet, black (available for a very short time in the mid-1990s): ....$10-$15

Rare green Batman test mold. **$NA**
(From the Johann Patek collection.)

Batman, Dark Knight (L to R): pointy ear version **$3-$6,** and rounded ear version **$1-$2.**

1960s Batman (L to R): no feet **$20-$30,** with feet **$10-$15,** and mid-1990s black short ears **$10-$15.**

Bear

Late 1990s, with feet
This dispenser uses the same head as the Icee Bear and the FAO Schwarz Bear, and was not available in the U.S.

Value: .... $10-$15

Unusual color variations of the late 1990s bear. **$10-$15**

Betsy Ross

1975 Bicentennial series, no feet

Value: ....$125-$150

Betsy Ross.
$125-$150

Scoops from the 2002 Bob the Builder series. **$1-$2**
(KP Photo)

Bob. **$2-$4**

Bob the Builder

2002, with feet

Value: .... $2-$4

Wendy, Pritchard the Cat, and Spud the Scarecrow from the Bob the Builder series. **$2-$4**

Boy and Boy with Cap

Mid-1960s to current, no feet and with feet

Many versions of the PEZ® Pal Boy have been produced through the years. One of the rarest is the brown-hair boy without hat used in a mid-1980s promotion for the movie *Stand By Me*. The dispenser is packaged with one pack of multi-flavor candy and a miniature version of the movie poster announcing the videocassette release and the quote, "If I could only have one food to eat for the rest of my life? That's easy, PEZ®. Cherry flavored PEZ®. No question about it." This dispenser must be sealed in original bag to be considered complete. Watch for reproduction hats.

Boy with blue cap, blond hair: ....$100-$125
Boy with red cap, blond hair:...$250-$300
Boy with blue cap, brown hair: ....$75-$100
Blond hair: ....$50-$75
Brown hair: ....$25-$35
Stand By Me (sealed in bag with mini-poster): ....$125-$150

Boy with Cap (blue) and blond hair. **$100-$125**

Boy with blond hair. **$50-$75**

Bozo the Clown

Early 1960s, no feet
This dispenser is usually die-cut on the side of the stem with a picture of Bozo and Butch. The non-die-cut stem is actually more difficult to find.

Die-cut stem: ....$175-$200
Plain stem: ....$185-$200

Bozo the Clown plain stem. **$185-$200**

Bratz

2005, with feet

Value: $1-$2 each

Bratz (L-R): Cloe, Jade, Yasmine, and Sasha. **$1-$2 each**

Bride and Groom (LIMITED EDITION)
Current, with feet
New limited edition Bride and Groom dispensers (mail order only).

Value: .... $20-$30 per set
African American variation (2004): .... $25-$35 per set

Limited Edition Bride and Groom. **$20-$30 per set**

Bride
Late 1970s, no feet
The Bride is a very rare and much desired piece by collectors. This dispenser, along with the Groom, was created for Robert and Claudia's wedding (relatives of a PEZ® executive) that took place October 6, 1978. They were used as place setting gifts and each guest received a set. The Bride is much harder to find than the Groom. It should be noted that the hair is different than the hair on the nurse.

Orange hair: .... $1800-$2000
Brown hair: .... $2000-$2200
Blonde hair: .... $2100-$2300

Bride, orange hair. **$1800-$2000**

Bubbleman

Mid-1990s, with feet

This dispenser was only available from PEZ® through a mail-in offer. The Bubbleman was the first set offered in this manner. They have the copyright date of 1992 on the dispenser, but didn't appear until the fall of 1996.

Value: .... $5 $10 each
Neon Bubbleman (1998): .... $3-$6 each
Crystal Bubbleman (1999): .... $3-$6 each
Glowing Bubbleman: .... $3-$6 each

Example of Crystal Bubbleman. **$3-$6**

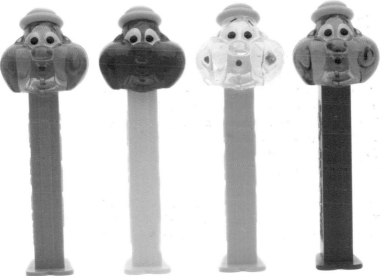

Crystal Bubbleman assortment. **$3-$6**

Additional examples of the Neon Bubbleman dispensers.

Neon Bubbleman dispensers. **$3-$6**

Glowing Bubbleman. Available through mail order only. **$10-$15**

Original Bubbleman dispensers. **$5-$10**

Bugs Bunny

Late 1970s to current, no feet and with feet

No feet: ....$15-$20
With feet, older-style head: ....$5-$10
Painted ears: ....$1-$2
Current: ....$1-$2

Recent Bugs Bunny dispenser. **$1-$2**

Bugs Bunny dispensers from the late 1970s (L to R): no feet **$15-$20,** with feet (2 examples) **$5-$10,** and painted ears **$1-$2**.

Bugz

Summer, 2000 with feet

The PEZ® Web site calls them Barney Beetle, Jumpin' Jack the grasshopper, Florence Flutterfly, Sam Snuffle the fly, Super Bee, Sweet Ladybird the ladybug, the Clumsy Worm, and Good-Natured Centipede. The Crystal Bugz pictured here are special ones found only through mail order or Wal-Mart Kids' connection candy stores.

Value: ....**$1-$2 each**
Crystal Bugz:...**$4-$6 each**

Caterpillar. **$1-$2**

The "smart bee" or baby bee, **$1-$2,** Crystal **$4-$6.**

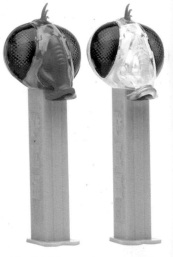

Beetle **$1-$2,** Grasshopper **$1-$2,** and Crystal Grasshopper **$4-$6.**

Fly **$1-$2,** and Crystal Fly **$4-$6.**

Flutterfly **$1-$2,** and Crystal Flutterfly **$4-$6.**

Beetle and Grasshopper. **$1-$2**

Caterpillar **$1-$2,** and Crystal Caterpillar **$4-$6.**

Sweet Ladybird **$1-$2,** Crystal Sweet Ladybird **$4-$6,** Clumsy Worm **$1-$2,** and Crystal Clumsy Worm **$4-$6.**

Flutterfly, Fly, and Bee. **$1-$2**

Bee **$1-$2,** and Crystal Bee **$4-$6.**

Bullwinkle

Early 1960s, no feet

Bullwinkle can be found with either a yellow or a brown stem—the brown is much harder to find.

Yellow stem:...$250-$275
Brown stem:..$275-$325

Bullwinkle, brown stem.
$275-$325

Bullwinkle, yellow stem.
$250-$275

Bundesrat Boy and Girl

2005, with feet

The Bundesrat is one of the five permanent constitutional organs of the Federal Republic of Germany. These dispensers were given away with a safety game for children in 2005. For some reason the girl seems to be easier to find than the boy.

Girl: ....$10-$15
Boy: ....$15-$20

Bundesrat Boy **$15-$20,** and Girl **$10-$15.**
(KP Photo)

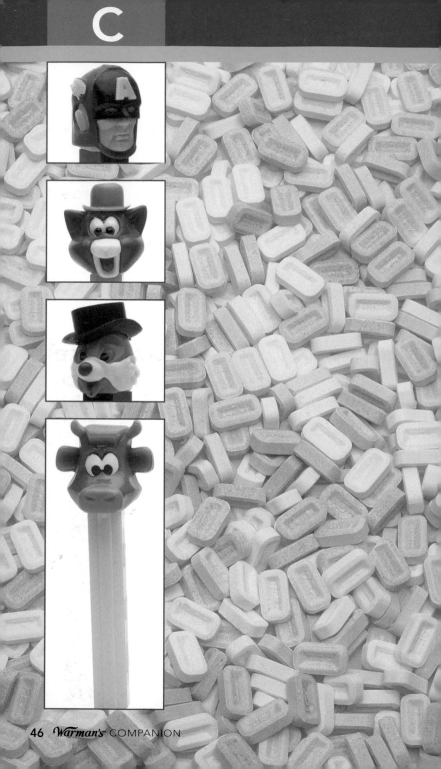

Camel (whistle)

No feet and with feet
The camel can be found with either a brown or a tan head.

No feet: ....$75-$100
With feet:...$50-$75

Camel, whistle with feet. **$50-$75**

Captain (Also known as Paul Revere)

Mid-1970s, no feet
This dispenser should have a sticker on the left side of his hat to be considered complete.

Value: .... **$150-$175**

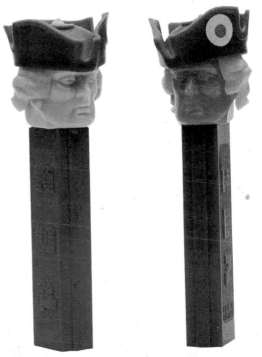

Captain, also known as Paul Revere. **$150-$175**

Captain America

Late 1970s, no feet

Captain America was produced with a black and a blue mask—the black mask is tougher to find.

Black mask: .... $100-$125
Blue mask: .... $85-$110

Captain America, black mask version (L) **$100-$125,** blue mask version (R) **$85-$110.**

Captain Hook

Late 1960s, no feet

A very rare softhead version of this dispenser was produced in the late 1970s, but never went into general production.

Value: ....$100-$140
Softhead: .... $3000+

Captain Hook. **$100-$140**

Cars the Movie

2006, with feet

Early versions of Mater (pictured far left) can be found with the entire engine area painted brown. The later and correct version only has the round air cleaner painted. Doc Hudson and Sally Porsche can be found without the trademark "Hudson Hornet" and "Porsche" on the base of the right side of the car.

Value: .... $1-$2 each

Cars the Movie (L-R): Mater, Lightning McQueen, Doc Hudson, and Sally Porsche.
$1-$2 ea
(KP Photo)

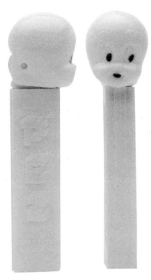

Casper, regular stem.
$150-$175

Casper

Late 1950s, no feet

No one is sure which licensed character first graced the top of a PEZ® dispenser. Some say it was Mickey Mouse, some say Popeye, and others say Casper. One story has it that Curt Allina, executive vice-president of PEZ® from 1953 to 1979, and Mr. Harvey, creator of Casper, had apartments in the same New York building in the 1950s. While living there the two developed a friendship and an agreement to use Harvey's character on the candy dispenser. The rest, as they say, is history.

Casper can be found with white, light blue, and light yellow stems as well as a die-cut version with a red or black sleeve.

Value: .... $150-$175
Die-cut stem: .... $200-$250

Cat with Derby (also known as Puzzy Cat)

Early 1970s, no feet

Several head and hat color combinations are available, as are many stem colors.

The blue hat version is the rarest, selling for twice that of other versions.

Value: .... $85-$95
Blue hat: .... $150-$175

Cat with Derby. **$85-$95**

Cat with Derby **$85-$95,** blue hat version **$150-$175.**

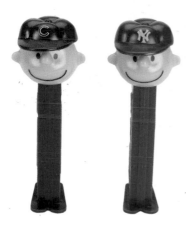

Charlie Brown Baseball Promos

2002-2003, with feet

2002 Chicago Cubs and 2003 New York Yankees sponsored by Verizon Wireless.

Value: .... **$20-$30 each**

Charlie Brown Baseball Promos. **$20-$30 each**
(KP Photo)

Chicken Little

2006, with feet

Value: .... **$1-$2**

Chicken Little (L-R): Abby, Chicken Little, and Fish out of water. **$1-$2**
(KP Photo)

Chicken Little: Golden Fish out of Water, a 2006 European movie promo. **$15-$20**
(KP Photo)

Chick in Egg

Early 1970s to current, no feet and with feet

The earliest versions of this popular dispenser have a brittle plastic eggshell with jagged points. The second version has a thin flexible plastic shell with more uniform points that resemble a saw blade. The third version, from the 1980s, has a much thicker shell, but with the same type of points as on the second version. The current version is also a thicker plastic, but there are fewer points on the shell and edges are more rounded.

Chick in Egg, no hat, no feet: ....$120-$150
Chick in Egg A, with hat, no feet: ....$100-$120
Chick in Egg B, with hat, no feet: ....$25-$35
Chick in Egg B, with feet: ....$2-$4
Chick in Egg C, with hat, no feet: ....$20-$30
Chick in Egg C, with hat, with feet: ....$5-$10
Chick in Egg D, with hat, with feet: ....$2-$3
Chick in Egg E, with hat, with feet (current): ....$1-$2

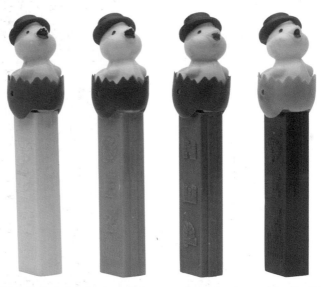

Chick in Egg B, with hat. This second version has a thin, flexible plastic shell with more uniform points that resemble a saw blade. **$25-$35**

Chick in Egg A, no hat, the oldest version. **$120-$150**

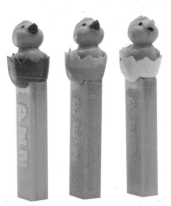

Three variations of the Chick in Egg, without hat. **$120-$150**
(From the Johann Patek collection.)

Chick in Egg A, with hat, old version with thin, brittle shell. Notice the steel pin. **$100-$120**

More recent versions of the Chick in Egg with hat from the 1980s to current. The dispenser on the far left is version B with feet **$2-$4,** version C with feet is next to that **$5-$10,** and the two on the right are version D with feet **$2-$3.**

Chick on Easter card. **$150-$200**
(From the Maryann Kennedy collection.)

Chip

Late 1970s, no feet and with feet
PEZ® only produced one half of the famous Disney chipmunk duo of Chip and Dale.

No feet: .... $75-$100
With feet: .... $50-$75

Chip, with feet. **$50-$75**

Chip, no feet.
$75-$100

Clown with Chin (Also known as Long Face Clown)

Mid-1970s, no feet
This dispenser can be found with many hair, hat, and nose color combinations.

Value: .... $85-$100

Additional color variations of Clown with Chin.
$85-$100

Clown with chin.
$85-$100

Clown with Collar

1960s, no feet

Value:................................. $60-$75

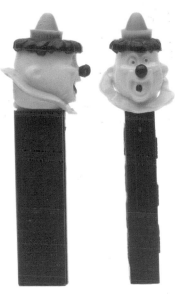

Clown with Collar. **$60-$75**

Clown (whistle)

No feet and with feet

No feet: ....$20-$35
With feet:................................$5-$10

Clown, whistle with feet. **$5-$10**

Coach's Whistle
No feet and with feet

No feet: ....$35-$50
With feet:..$1-$3

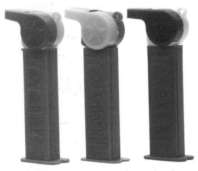

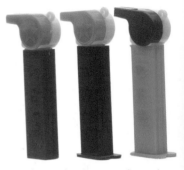

Coach's Whistle, with feet. **$1-$3.**

Coach's Whistle, no feet **$35-$50,** and with feet **$1-$3.**

Coach's Whistle 2005: Can be found in 6 different colors **$1-$2.**
(KP Photo)

Cockatoo

Mid-1970s, no feet and with feet
Several head and beak color combinations are available. The peach-colored beak is harder to find and worth slightly more than other colors.

No feet: .... **$65-$85**
With feet: .... **$45-$65**

Cockatoo, no feet.
$65-$85

Additional color variations of Cockatoo no feet. **$65-$85**

Cockta Trucks

2005, with feet
Cockta is a soft drink in Slovenia.

Value: ....**$10-$15**

Cockta Trucks. **$10-$15**
(KP Photo)

Cool Cat

Early 1980s, no feet and with feet

No feet: .... $65-$85
With feet:.................... $45-$65

Cool Cat, with feet. **$45-$65**

Cow A

Early 1970s, no feet
There are many different color variations of the head. The green head is a rare variation and sells for two to three times as much as other versions.

Value: ....$125-$150

Cow A. **$125-$150**
(Green head from the Maryann Kennedy collection.)

There are many color variations of the Cow A head. **$100-$125**

Additional color variations of Cow A. **$100-$125**

Cow A, rare brown variation. **$NA**
(From the Johann Patek collection.)

Cow B

Mid-1970s, no feet

Many different color combinations can be found. The same mold was used to make the head for the Yappy Dog.

Value: ....$85-$120

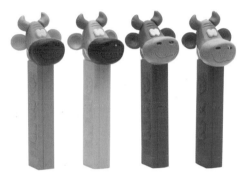

Variations of the Cow B dispenser. **$85-$120**
(Green and yellow Cow from the Maryann Kennedy collection.)

Cowboy

Early 1970s, no feet

Value: .... **$200-$250**

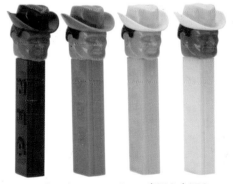

Cowboy. **$200-$250**

Cowboy variations. **$200-$250**
(From the Johann Patek collection.)

Crazy Animals

Released fall 1999, with feet
Originally not sold in the U.S. Later available in refill bags.
Four animals: Frog, Shark, Octopus, and Camel.

Value: ....$1-$3

Crazy Animals Shark, Octopus, and Camel. **$1-$3**

Crazy Animals Frog. **$1-$3**

Crazy Fruit Series

Mid-1970s, no feet
The Orange first appeared in the mid-1970s, followed by the Pear and Pineapple in the late 1970s. The Pineapple is the hardest of the three to find, followed by the Pear then the Orange. The Lemon was made as production sample, but never produced.

Orange: ....$200-$250
Pear: ....$800-$1200
Pineapple: ....$2500-$3000
Lemon: .... $8000+

The ultra-rare Lemon Crazy Fruit dispenser—this is a production sample; the dispenser was never produced. **$8000+**
(From the Dora Dwyer collection.)

Crazy Fruit series (L to R) Pear **$800-$1200,** Orange **$200-$250,** and Pineapple **$2500-$3000.**

(Pear and Pineapple from the Maryann Kennedy collection.)

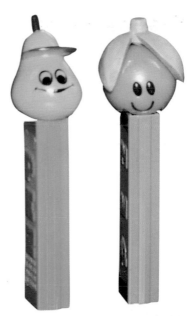

Crazy Fruit series Pear **$800-$1000,** and Orange **$200-$250.**

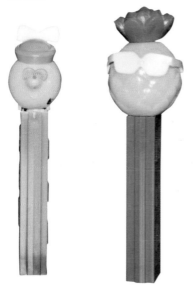

Crazy Fruit series Lemon (L) **$3000+,** and Pineapple (R) **$2500-$3000.**

(From the Dora Dwyer collection.)

Ultra-rare short stem Pineapple (L) **$NA,** and regular version (R) **$2500-$3000.**

(From the Johann Patek collection.)

Crocodile

Mid-1970s, no feet

Can be found in several shades of green and even in purple. The purple version sells for about twice as much as green dispensers.

Value (green head crocodiles): .... $100-$125

Crocodile, green head. **$100-$125**

Crystal Ball Dispenser

Sold through a 2002 mail-in offer for $15.95. It has tiny silver sparkles in the stem and base. The first 2500 were made by mistake using silver stars, the remaining production will have blue stars.

Value: .... $10-$15

Crystal Ball Dispenser, with blue stars. **$10-$15**

Crystal Ball Dispenser, with silver stars. **$10-$15**

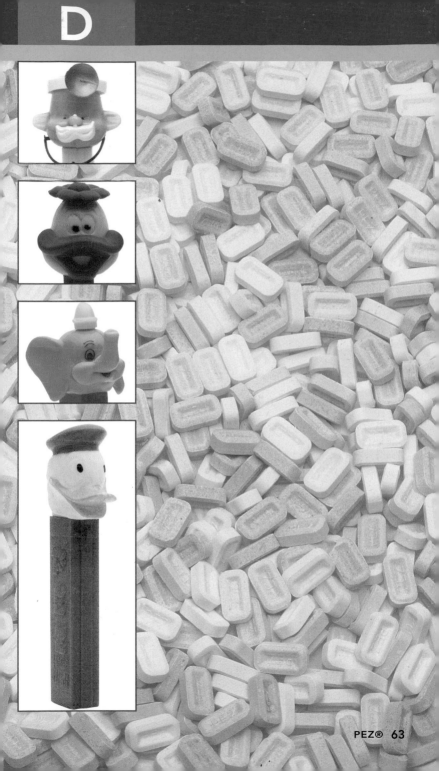

Daffy Duck

Late 1970s to current, no feet and with feet

Many versions of Daffy have been produced. The first version with separate eye pieces is the toughest to find.

Daffy Duck A (separate eye pieces): ....$25-$30
Daffy Duck B (painted eyes and tongue): ....$15-$20
Daffy Duck C (with feet, older-style head): ....$5-$8
Daffy Duck D (current style): ....$1-$2

Current Daffy Duck. **$1-$2**

Daffy Duck grouping, (L) version is the toughest to find with separate eye pieces and is valued at **$25-$30.**

Daisy Duck

Late 1990s, with feet

Value: .... $1-$2

Daisy Duck. **$1-$2**

Dalmatian Pup

Late 1970s, no feet and with feet

No feet: .... $75-$95
With feet: .... $60-$75

Dalmatian Pup, with feet. **$60-$75**

Daniel Boone

Mid-1970s, no feet

Value: .... $175-$200

Daniel Boone, no feet. **$175-$200**

Die-Cuts

Early 1960s

A Die-Cut dispenser is one in which a design is cut into the side of the stem. The cutout usually reveals an inner sleeve of a different color. Several dispensers were made with a die-cut stem in the 1960s.

Casper: .... $250-$275
Donald Duck: .... $175-$200
Mickey Mouse: .... $125-$175
Easter Rabbit: .... $350-$500
Bozo:... $175-$200

Bozo, die-cut dispenser.
$175-$200

Mickey Mouse (L) **$125-$175,** and Easter Rabbit (R) die-cut dispenser **$350-$500.**

Casper (L) **$250-$275,** and Donald Duck (R) die-cut dispenser **$175-$200.**

Dinosaurs

Early 1990s, with feet

The dinosaurs were first released in Europe in the early 1990s and were known as the "Trias Family"—Brutus, Titus, Chaos, and Venesia. Shortly thereafter, they were introduced to the United States as "Pez-a-Saurs."

Value: ....$1-$2

She-Saur dinosaur. **$1-$2**

Fly-Saur, He-Saur, and L-Saur. **$1-$2**

Crystal Dinosaur

1999, with feet

Only available through PEZ® mail-in offer.

Value: .... $3-$5

Crystal Dinosaur. **$3-$5**

Additional Crystal Dinosaurs. **$3-$5**

Disney Princesses

2005-2006, with feet

The 2006 editions to the princess line are Aurora from *Sleeping Beauty* and Ariel from *The Little Mermaid*. Snow White will be reissued in 2007 with a Disney DVD release.

Value: .... **$1-$2 each**

Disney Princesses, Aurora and Ariel. **$1-$2** each
(KP Photo)

Disney Princesses (2005): Jasmine from *Aladdin*, Belle from *Beauty and the Beast*, and Cinderella. **$1-$2**
(KP Photo)

Disney Softheads

Late 1970s

These dispensers are ultra rare and were never sold to the public. The few that are known to exist have come from former employees of PEZ®. There are six dispensers in this group: Pluto, Donald Duck, Goofy, Captain Hook, Dumbo, and Mickey Mouse.

Value: ....$3000+ ea

Mickey Mouse, Pluto, and Goofy Softheads. **$3000+**
(From the Dora Dwyer collection.)

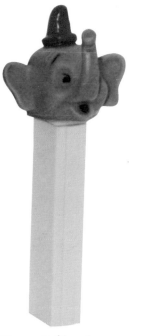

Disney Softheads were never put on stems. The ones shown here are for display purposes only. Dumbo Softhead. **$3000+**
(From the Dora Dwyer collection.)

Goofy, Donald, and Captain Hook Softheads. **$3000+**
(From the Dora Dwyer collection.)

Doctor and Nurse

Early 1970s, no feet

Both of these dispensers are available in several versions. The doctor comes with or without hair on either a blue, white, or yellow stem. The nurse can be found with brown, reddish orange, yellow, or blonde hair on several different stem colors. There is also a variation in her hat: one is a solid white and the other is an opaque or milky-white, semi-transparent color that is usually only found in dispensers that came from Canada.

Doctor with hair: ....$150-$250
Doctor without hair: ....$100-$125
Nurse with yellow hair: ....$150-$200
Nurse with brown hair: ....$150-$250

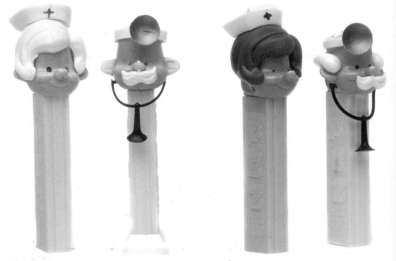

Nurse with yellow hair **$150-$250,** and Bald Doctor **$100-$125.**

Nurse with brown hair **$150-$250,** and Doctor with hair **$150-$200.**

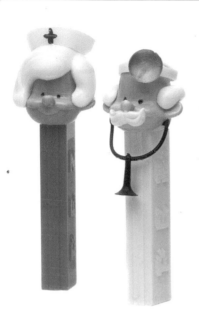

Nurse with blonde hair **$150-$250,** and Doctor with hair **$150-$200.**

Nurse with reddish-orange hair. **$150-$200**

Dog (whistle)
No feet and with feet

No feet: ....$30-$40
With feet: $20 $30

Dog, whistle, no feet. **$30-$40**

Donald Duck

Early 1960s to current, no feet and with feet

Many versions of Donald have been made over the years. Version D, which has holes in the beak, was also used as the head of the Uncle Scrooge McDuck dispenser. An extremely rare "softhead" version also exists, but these never made it to general production.

Version A, (original-early 1960s) sharp, defined feathers, no feet: ....$20-$30

Version B, a remake of A with the feathers less defined on top of head, no feet:................$15-$25

Version C, 2 hinge-holes on the side of the head, milky white plastic head, early-mid-1970s, no feet and with feet: ....$15-$25

Version D, 2 hinge-hole on the side of the head, hole in beak, no feet and with feet:..$10-$20

Version E, produced in the 1980s, came with both light and dark blue eyes: ....$2-$4

Version F, late 1990s version, the beak is open: ....$1-$2

Softhead version:... $3000+

Donald Duck, version E with light eyes. **$2-$4**

Donald Duck, version E with dark blue eyes (L), and version F (R) **$1-$2.**

Donald Duck, original version (L)
$20-$30, version B (R) **$15-$25.**

Donald Duck, version C (L) **$15-$25,** and version B (R) **$15-$25.**

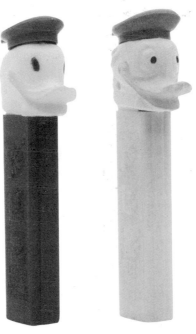

Donkey (whistle)
No feet and with feet

No feet: .... $35-$45
With feet: .... $5-$10

Donkey, whistle with feet. **$5-$10**

Dopey
Late 1960s, no feet

Value: ....$200-$225

Dopey. **$200-$225**

Droopy

Early 1980s, no feet and with feet
This dispenser was not released in the U.S. Two versions were made— one with painted ears and one with movable ears.

Painted ears: ....$5-$10
Moveable ears: ....$25-$30

Droopy, with painted ears. **$5-$10**

Droopy, with movable ears. **$25-$30**

Duck (whistle)

No feet and with feet

No feet: .... $45-$55
With feet:... $30-$40

Duck, whistle with feet. **$30-$40**

Duck with Flower

Early 1970s, no feet
Many head, flower, and beak color combinations can be found. Black, orange, and yellow are the hardest head colors to find and usually sell for twice as much as other color variations.

Value: .... $100-$125
Yellow head: .... $150-$175
Black or orange head:...... $200-$250

Duck with flower, versions with yellow head **$150-$175**, green head **$100-$125**, and orange head **$200-$250**.

Duck with flower. **$100-$125**

Duck Nephews

Originals are from the late 1970s, footed versions are from the late 1980s to 1990s. Variations can be found of this dispenser with large and small pupils. The early version is also known as "Duck Child" and was only produced with blue or green hats; the later versions were produced with red hats, in addition to blue and green.

Originals: .... $30-$40
With feet:............................ $5-$10

Duck Nephews, original version. **$30-$40**

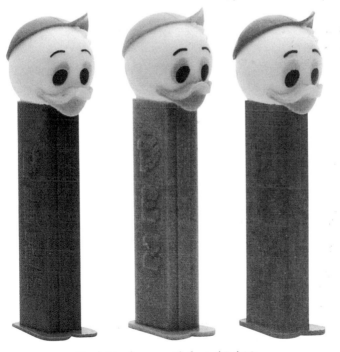

Duck Nephews, with feet. **$5-$10**

Ducktails

Early 1990s, with feet

Gyro Gearloose:	.............$5-$8
Bouncer Beagle:	.............$5-$8
Webagail or Webby:	......$5-$8

Ducktails Gyro Gearloose, Bouncer Beagle, and Webagail (or Webby) **$5-$8**.

Dumbo

Late 1970s, no feet and with feet

No feet:	....$50-$60
With feet:	....$30-$50
A very rare softhead version also exists:	.... $3000+

Dumbo, no feet. **$50-$60**.

Dumbo, with feet (L) **$30-$50**, and no feet **$50-$60**.

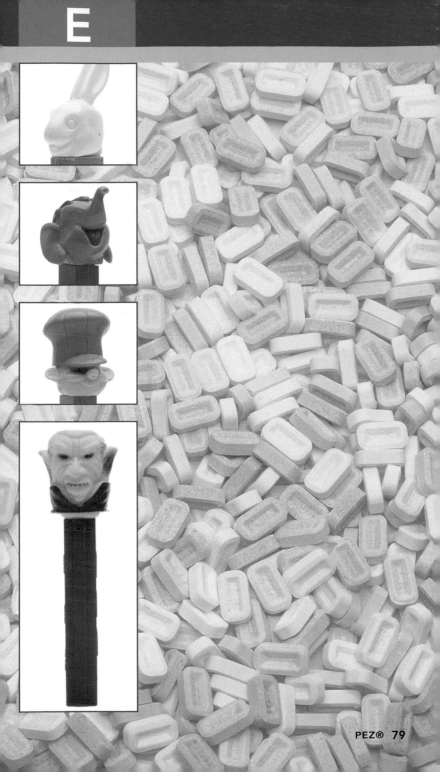

E.T.

2002, with feet

Value: .... $2-$4

E.T. **$2-$4**

Easter 2004

2004, with feet

Chick in Egg, Pink Bunny, Baby Face in Egg, and Lamb.

Value: .... **$1-$2 each**

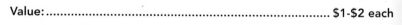

Easter 2004. **$1-$2 ea**

Easter Bunny

1950s to current, no feet and with feet

Bunny A, no feet, 1950s: ....$200-$250
Bunny B, no feet, 1950s: ....$250-$300
Fat Ear Bunny, no feet, 1960s-1970s: ....$25-$40
Fat Ear Bunny, with feet: ....$10-$20
Bunny D, 1990s: ....$2-$4
Bunny E, (current): ....$1-$2

Bunny B from the 1950s is a tough find. **$250-$300**
(From the Maryann Kennedy collection.)

Easter Bunny. (L to R) Bunny A **$200-$250,** Fat Ear Bunny, no feet
$25-$40, Bunny D **$2-$4,** and Bunny E **$1-$2.**

Fat Ear bunnies, with feet (L) **$10-$20,** and no feet (R) **$25-$40.**

Fat Ear Bunny variations, no feet. **$25-$40**

eBay Employee Dispenser

2000, with feet

This glow in the dark dispenser was given to all employees who worked at eBay as a bonus. Initially these dispensers were selling in the $200+ range but prices have come down.

Value: ....$50-$75

eBay Employee Dispenser. **$50-$75**
(KP Photo)

Eerie Spectres (Also known as Softhead Monsters)

Late 1970s, no feet

This group is very popular among collectors. There are two variations for each character—"Made in Hong Kong" and "Hong Kong." These are the two different markings used on the back of the head with the "Hong Kong" mark being a bit harder to find. There is also a very distinct difference in face color between the two. The stems of these dispensers are always marked "Made in the USA." The six characters in the series are Air Spirit, Diabolic, Scarewolf, Spook, Vamp, and Zombie.

"Made in Hong Kong": ....$200-$250
"Hong Kong": ....$225-$275

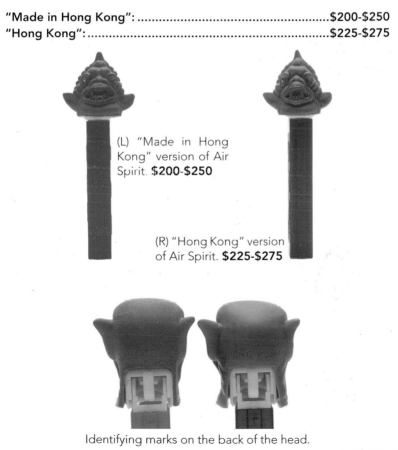

(L) "Made in Hong Kong" version of Air Spirit. **$200-$250**

(R) "Hong Kong" version of Air Spirit. **$225-$275**

Identifying marks on the back of the head.

(L) "Hong Kong" Vamp. **$225-$250**

(R) "Made in Hong Kong" version of Vamp. **$200-$250**

"Hong Kong" Zombie. **$225-$275**

"Made in Hong Kong" Zombie. **$200-$250**

(L) "Made in Hong Kong" Diabolic. **$200-$250**

(R) "Hong Kong" Diabolic. **$225-$250**

Hand-painted heads can vary greatly in detail.

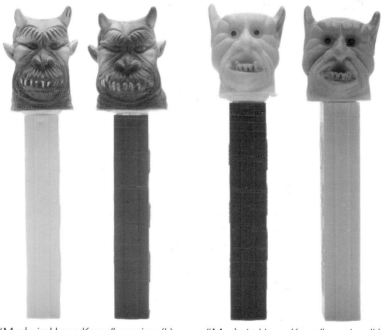

"Made in Hong Kong" version (L) **$200-$250**, and "Hong Kong" Spook (R) **$225-$275.**

"Made in Hong Kong" version (L) **$200-$250**, and "Hong Kong" Scarewolf (R) **$225-$275.**

Elephant (Also known as Circus Elephant or Big Top Elephant)

Early 1970s, no feet

There are three different variations to the elephant regarding its head gear—flat hat, pointy hat, and hair. The elephant came in many different color combinations, some of which, such as the pink head variation, are tough to find.

Flat hat: ....$100-$125
Pointy hat: ....$125-$150
Hair: ....$150-$175

More color variations for elephant with pointy hat. **$125-$150**

Elephant, with hair. **$150-$175**

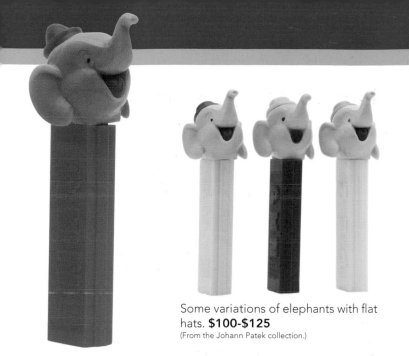

Some variations of elephants with flat hats. **$100-$125**
(From the Johann Patek collection.)

Elephant, with pointy hat. **$125-$150**

Elephant, with flat hat. **$100-$125**
(Pink elephant from the Maryann Kennedy collection.)

Emergency Heroes

2003, with feet

Fireman, Construction Worker, Army Soldier, Scuba Diver, Jet Pilot, Nurse, Policeman, Police K-9, and Policewoman. The Fireman and Construction Worker have African-American variations.

Value: .... $1-$2 each
African-American variations: .... $5-$10 each

Emergency Heroes, Fireman and Construction Worker. **$1-$2 ea**
(KP Photo)

Emergency Heroes (L-R): Army Soldier, Scuba Diver, Jet Pilot, and Nurse. **$1-$2 ea**
(KP Photo)

Emergency Heroes (L-R): Policeman, Police K-9, and Policewoman. **$1-$2 ea**
(KP Photo)

Engineer
Mid-1970s, no feet

Value:..$175-$200

Engineer. **$175-$200**

Fireman

Early 1970s, no feet

The Fireman was available with a dark moustache. White moustache rarities must be sealed in the package to be considered a variation. Notice the light gray badge variation on the fireman on the far right.

Darker badge:......................................$75-$100
Lighter badge: ....$200-$250

Fireman with darker badge. **$75-$90**

Fireman with darker badge (L) **$75-$100**, and lighter badge version (R) **$200-$250**.

Fishman

Mid-1970s, no feet

The Fishman used the same mold as the Creature from the Black Lagoon, which was done as part of a Universal Studios Monsters series. The Creature was all green whereas the Fishman came with either a green or a black head and various colored stems.

Value: ....$175-$200

The all-green version of Fishman is known as the "Creature from the Black Lagoon." **$250-$300**

Various Fishman dispensers. **$175-$200**

Flintstones

Mid-1990s, with feet

Series includes Barney Rubble, Dino, Fred Flintstone, and Pebbles Flintstone.

Value: .... $1-$2

Fred Flintstone. **$1-$2**

Barney Rubble, Pebbles Flintstone, and Dino. **$1-$2**

Foghorn Leghorn

Early 1980s, no feet and with feet
Foghorn Leghorn can be found with either a yellow or an orange beak.

No feet: ....$85-$100
With feet:..$65-$85

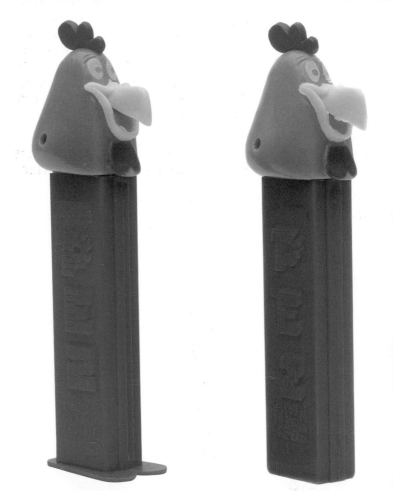

Foghorn Leghorn, with feet.
$65-$85

Foghorn Leghorn, no feet.
$85-$100

Football Player

Mid-1960s, no feet

This dispenser can be found in either red or blue and will either have a tape strip on the helmet (as shown) or a plastic strip that snaps on the front and back of the helmet. This version is very tough to find. The blank side of the stem with the triangle allowed kids to customize the dispenser with a pennant-shaped sticker of their favorite team.

Tape-strip Helmet:. $150-$175
Snap-on Stripe: ....$250+

Football Player, with original vending box. **$200-$250**

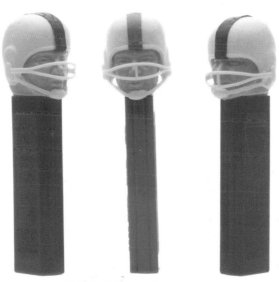

Football Player dispensers.

Frog (whistle)
No feet and with feet

No feet: ....$40-$50
With feet:...$30-$40

Frog, whistle, no feet. **$40-$50**

Football Sport Looney Tunes
2006, with feet
European Release

Value: .... $3-$4 each

Football Sport Looney Tunes: Taz, Tweety, and Bugs Bunny. **$3-$4**
(KP Photo)

Funky Faces

2003, with feet
There are 13 different "Funky Faces" to collect.

Value: ....$1-$2 ea

Funky Faces (L-R): Toothy Smile, Angry Face, Embarrassed Face, and Smiley with Tongue. **$1-$2**
(KP Photo)

Funky Faces (L-R): Kissy Face, Smiling with Eyelashes, Crying Face, and Baby Face. **$1-$2**
(KP Photo)

Funky Faces (L-R): Open Smile, Cool Sunglasses Smile, Nerdy Egghead, Smiley Face, and Winking Smiley Face. **$1-$2**
(KP Photo)

FX Toy Show

2005, with feet
The five promotional dispensers (shown here) could be purchased at the show for $5.95 each. There were also three different print color variations: One was given to dealers/exhibitors, another to the first 500 people through the door, and the other to people purchasing a 3-day show pass.

Set of five dispensers: ..$30-$50
Color variations: ......$40-$75 ea

FX Toy Show, set of five. **$30-$50**
(KP Photo)

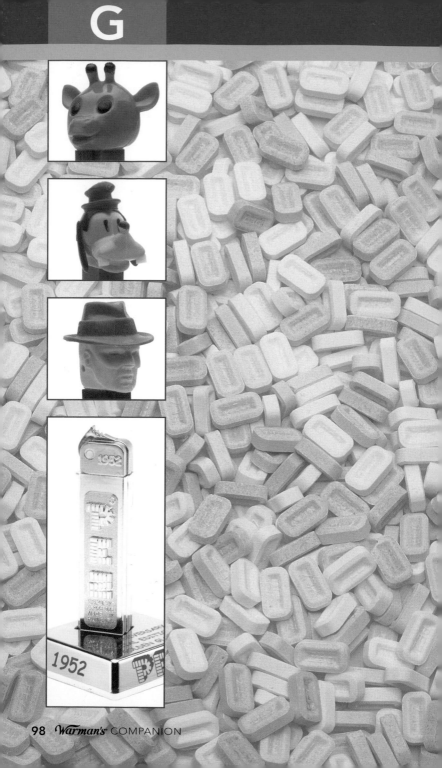

Garfield

1990s, with feet

Two series featuring the comic strip character Garfield have been produced—the first in the early 1990s, the second in the late 1990s. The first series includes Garfield, Garfield with teeth, Garfield with visor, Arlene, and Nermal. The second series includes Garfield, Chef Garfield, Sleepy Garfield, Aviator Garfield, and Odie.

First series: .... $2-$3 each
Second series:............................... $1-$2 each

A rare test mold version of Garfield. **$NA**
(From the Johann Patek collection.)

Garfield, first series Garfield, Garfield with teeth, and Garfield with visor. **$2-$3**

Garfield, first series Arlene and Nermal. **$2-$3**

Garfield, second series. (L to R) Garfield, Chef Garfield, Sleepy Garfield, Aviator Garfield, and Odie. **$1-$2**

Giraffe

Mid-1970s, no feet
This is one of the tougher animal dispensers to find.

Value: ....**$175-$200**

Giraffe. **$175-$200**

Girl

Early 1970s, no feet and with feet
The Girl can be found with either
blonde or yellow hair.

No feet: .... $25-$35
With feet: .... $5-$10

Another version of Girl, no feet.
$25-$35

Girl, no feet. **$25-$35**

Golden Glow

This dispenser was offered only as a mail-in premium and is tough to find with finish in good condition—tarnish spots are common.

Value: ....$85-$125

New Golden Glow 50th anniversary dispenser. **$20-$25**

Newer Golden Glow and Silver Glow regulars. **$85-$125**
(From the Johann Patek collection.)

Vintage Golden Glows. The round base is the older of the two **$85-$125 (with bases $200-$300).**
(From the Johann Patek collection.)

Goofy

1970s to current, no feet and with feet

Several Goofy dispensers have been produced over the years. Versions A, B, and C can be found with several face color variations.

Goofy A, removable ears, teeth and nose, no feet: ....$30-$45

Goofy B, removable ears and teeth, no feet:........................$25-$35

Goofy C, removable ears, no feet:.......................................$25-$35

Goofy C, with feet: ....$15-$25

Goofy D, late 1980s, green hat, with feet: ....$2-$5

Goofy E, current: ....$1-$2

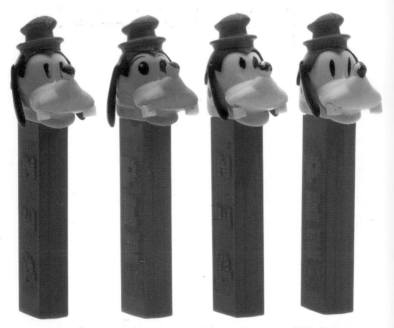

Goofy, version B with several face variations. **$25-$35**

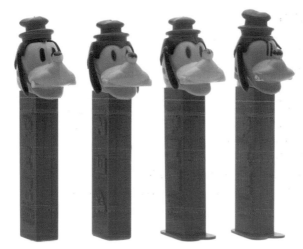

Goofy, version C with several face color variations. Shown are both types, no feet **$25-$35**, and with feet **$15-$25.**

Goofy, version D (L) **$2-$5**, and version E (R) **$1-$2.**

Unusual variations of Goofy. **$NA**
(From the Johann Patek collection.)

Green Hornet

Late 1960s, no feet

The Green Hornet was produced in two different versions—one with a small hat and the other with a larger hat. The hat can be found in either brown or gray.

Version A (smaller hat): .... $200-$225
Version B (larger hat): .... $175-$200

Green Hornet, version A with smaller hat. **$200-$225**

Close-up of the Green Hornet version B head.

Green Hornet, version B with larger hat. **$175-$200**

Green Hornet variations with smaller hat. **$200-$225**

Gorilla

Mid-1970s, no feet
This dispenser was produced with a black or brown head.

Value:....................................**$80-$95**

Two examples of the Gorilla. **$80-$95**

Groom

Late 1970s, no feet
A rare dispenser from the October 6, 1978 wedding of Robert and Claudia (relatives of a PEZ® executive).

Value:............... **$500-$700**

The very rare Groom dispenser.
$500-$700

Gundam

2005, with feet

Gundam is an animated series in Japan where the characters are space pilots who protect the earth from the evil Earth Sphere Alliance.

Loose: ....$5-$8
Mint-in-box: ....$8-$10

Gundam, Char's Zaku MS-065. **$8-$10**

Gundam, Zaku 2 MS-06F. **$8-$10**

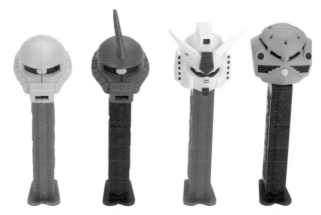

Gundam, Japanese release (L-R): Zaku 2 MS-06F, Char's Zaku MS-065, Gundam RX-78-2, and Z-Gock MSM-07. **$5-$8**

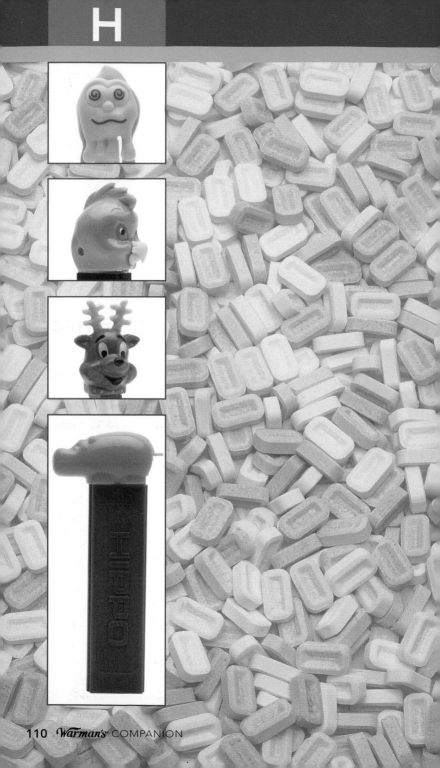

Halloween Black Cat

2006, with feet
Newest edition to the Halloween series. The stem glows in the dark.

Value:...$1-$2

Halloween Black Cat. **$1-$2**
(KP Photo)

Halloween Crystal Series

1999, with feet
This series was only available through a PEZ® mail-in offer. The series includes a Jack-o-Lantern and three different ghosts.

Value:.. $3-$5 each

Halloween Crystal
series Jack-o-
Lantern. **$3-$5**

Halloween Crystal series ghosts. **$3-$5**

Halloween Ghosts

Late 1990s, with feet

This non-glowing series was available in the U.S. for only a couple of years. Characters include: Naughty Neil, Slimy Sid, and Polly Pumpkin. These do not glow in the dark.

Value: ....$1-$2 ea

Halloween ghosts. **$1-$2**

Halloween 2005

with feet

Four glow-in-the-dark dispensers were released, Skull or "Toti" as referred to in the European sales catalog, Pumpkin, Witch, and Mummy.

Value: ....$1-$2 ea

Halloween 2005 (L-R): Skull, Pumpkin, Witch, and Mummy. **$1-$2**
(KP Photo)

Halloween Glowing Ghosts

Late 1990s, with feet

This glowing version first sold only in Europe, not released in the U.S. assortment until 2002. Characters include: Happy Henry, Naughty Neil, Slimy Sid, and Polly Pumpkin.

Value: ....$1-$2 each

Halloween Glowing Ghost Happy Henry. **$1-$2**

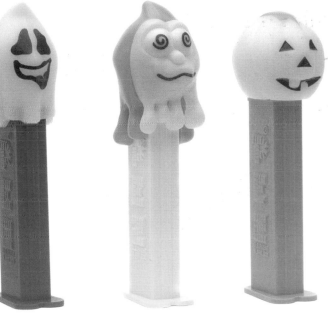

Halloween Glowing Ghosts Naughty Neil, Slimy Sid, and Polly Pumpkin. **$1-$2**

Halloween Glowing Ghost Polly Pumpkin glowing in the dark.

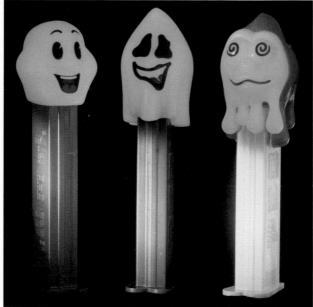

Additional Halloween Glowing Ghosts with the lights out.

Hello Kitty

2005-2006, with feet

2005 Regular issues:	$1-$2 ea
2005 Crystal issues from Japan:	$3-$5 ea
2006 Tin set:	$15-$20

Hello Kitty 2005 (L-R): Aloha Kitty, Hello Kitty with rabbit, Hello Kitty, and My Melodie. **$1-$2**
(KP Photo)

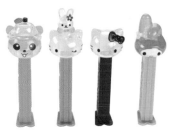

Crystal Hello Kitty (L-R): Kuririn, Hello Kitty with rabbit, Hello Kitty, and My Melodie. **$3-$5**
(KP Photo)

Hello Kitty tin set, crystal head version offered in this lunch box tin set. **$15-$20**
(KP Photo)

Hello Kitties

2006, with feet
European release. Stenciled stem crystal head.

Value: .... **$5-$7**

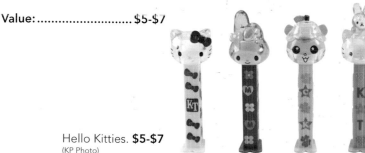

Hello Kitties. **$5-$7**
(KP Photo)

Henry Hawk

Early 1980s, no feet and with feet

No feet: ....$80-$100
With feet:...$60-$75

Henry Hawk, with feet. **$60-$75**

Hippo

Early 1970s, no feet

Among the rarest of the animal dispensers, the hippo was not released in the United States and is very difficult to find. The Hippo is unusual in that it has an entire body on top of the stem, rather than just a head.

Value: ....$700-$900

The Hippo was not released in the U.S., and is very difficult to find. **$700-$900**

Holiday 2002

With feet:..$1-$2

Holiday 2002 Santa, Snowman, Winter Bear, Elf, Reindeer. **$1-$2**

Holiday Clear Crystal Christmas Set (2005): Reindeer, Santa, Snowman, and Elf. Mail order set from Pez.com, **$4-$6 ea.**

Holiday Crystal Series

1999, with feet

This series was only available through a PEZ® mail-in offer. The series includes Santa, Snowman, Witch, and Skull.

Value: .... **$3-$5 each**

Holiday Crystal Series Witch and Skull. **$3-$5**

Holiday Crystal Series Santa and Snowman. **$3-$5**

Crystal Holiday Polar Bear. **$5-$8 each**
(KP Photo)

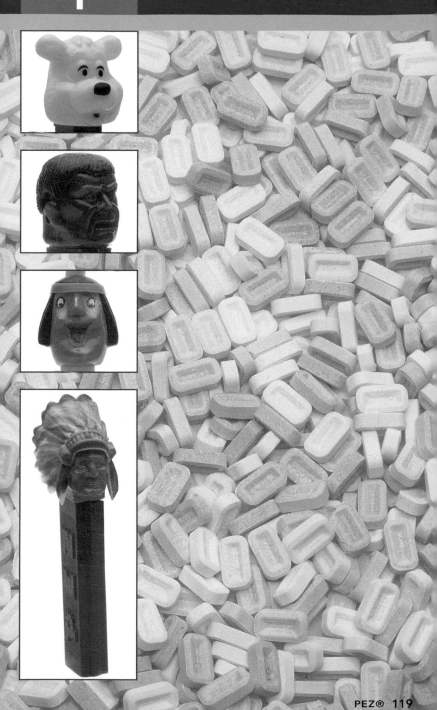

Ice Age 2: The Meltdown

2006, with feet

Based on the popular motion picture.

Value: .... $1-$2 each

Scrat, Manny, Diego, and Sid. **$1-$2**
(KP Photo)

Icee Bear

1990s, with feet

The earlier version of Icee Bear was not issued in the U.S. The version on the far right made its debut in the 1999 Christmas assortment. It was revised in 2002.

Early version: .... $5-$10 each
Far right: .... $1-$3
Current: .... $1-$2

Icee Bear, early version. **$5-$10**

1999 Christmas assortment Icee Bear. **$1-$3**

Incredibles

2004, with feet
U.S. released have masks, European releases do not.

With masks: ....$1-$2 ea
Without masks: ....$5-$8 ea
Golden Jack Jack: ....$10-$15

Incredibles U S. release (L-R): Dash, Helen Parr, Bob Parr, and Jack Jack. **$1-$2**
(KP Photo)

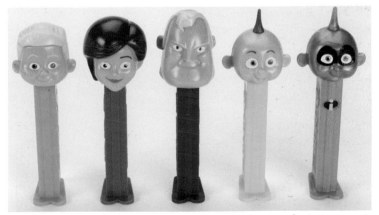

Incredibles European release (L-R): Dash, Helen Parr, Bob Parr, Jack Jack **$5-$8**, Golden Jack Jack (European movie promo) **$10-$15**.
(KP Photo)

Incredible Hulk

Late 1970s, no feet and with feet
The Incredible Hulk dispenser has been produced
in varying shades of green.

Dark green, no feet: ....$40-$50
Light green, no feet: ....$45-$55
Light green, with feet: ....$3-$5
With teeth (current version,
released 1999): ....$1-$2

1999 version of the
Incredible Hulk, light
green with feet. **$1-$2**

Rare white eye version
of the Incredible Hulk,
dark green no feet.
$NA
(From the Johann Patek collection.)

Incredible Hulk, (L to R) dark green **$40-$50**, light green no feet **$45-$55,** and light green with feet **$3-$5.**

Indian (whistle)

With feet

Value: ....$25-$35

Indian, whistle. **$25-$35**

Indian Brave

Early-1970s, no feet

Value: ....$150-$175

Indian Brave. **$150-$175**

Indian Chief

Early 1970s, no feet

The swirled headdress combinations are virtually endless. It is rumored the plastic used to make the headdress was molded from the ground-up and re-melted remains of unsold Make-a-Face dispensers.

Value: .... $125-$150
White headdress: .... $100-$125

Indian Chief. **$125-$150**

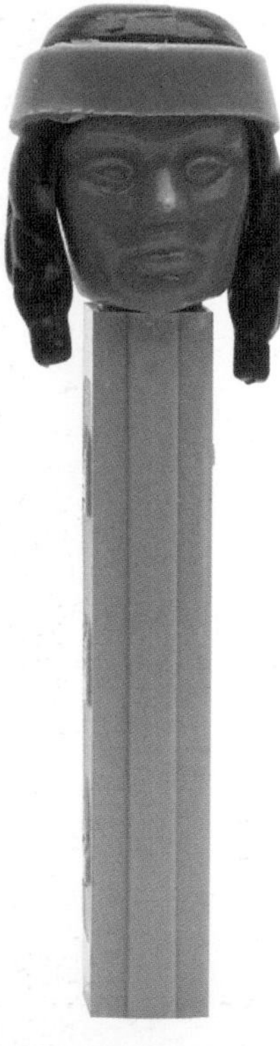

Indian Maiden

Mid-1970s, no feet

Value: ....$125-$150

Indian Maiden. **$125-$150**

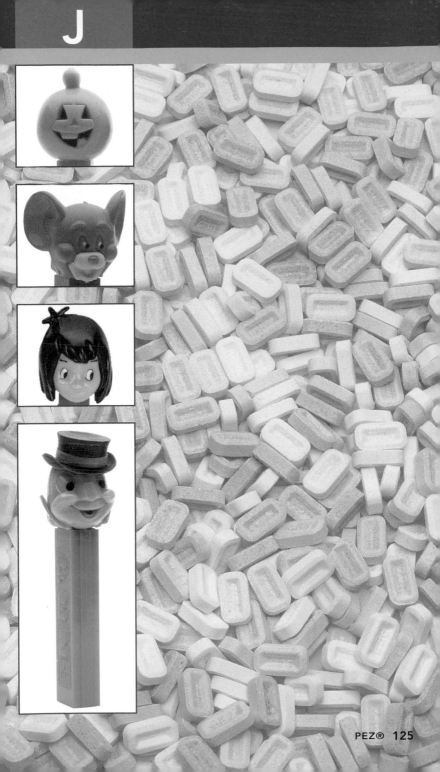

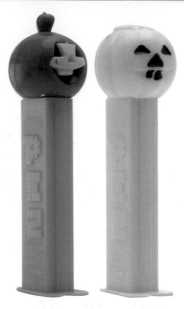

Jack-o-Lantern
1980s, no feet and with feet

Version A, die-cut face,
no feet: .... $20-$25
Version A, with feet: .... $10-$15
Version B: .... $2-$3
Version C: .... $1-$2
Version D glows in the dark
(current): .... $1-$2

Hard-to-find two-tone Jack-o-Lantern. **$NA**
(From the Johann Patek collection.)

Jack-o-Lantern, (L to R) version A no feet **$20-$25**, version A with feet **$10-$15**, version B **$2-$3**, and version C **$1-$2.**

Jerry

Early 1980s to current, no feet and with feet
One half of MGM's famous cat and mouse duo. Not released in the U.S. There are many variations of this dispenser.

No feet:	$30-$40
Thin Feet:	$5-$10
Multi-piece face:	$10-$15
With feet:	$4-$8
Current:	$2-$3

Another variation of the multi-piece-faced Jerry. **$10-$15**

Variation of the multi-piece-faced Jerry. **$10-$15**

Jerry, (L to R) no feet **$30-$40**, thin feet **$5-$10**, and multi-piece face **$10-$15**.

Jerry, with feet (L) **$4-$8**, and current release (R) **$2-$3.**

Rare ear insert versions of Jerry and Tuffy. **$NA**
(From the Johann Patek collection.)

Jeffrey the Bunny

2004, with feet

A retail candy store in New York City has immortalized its famous chocolate bunny mascot "Jeffrey" as a PEZ® dispenser.

Value: ....$4-$6
MOC:.................................$5-$8

Dylans Candy Bar. **$4-$6** loose, **$5-$8 MOC**
(KP Photo)

Jiminy Cricket

Early 1970s, no feet

With many small pieces making up his costume, Jiminy Cricket is a tough dispenser to find complete.

Value:..$200-$250

Jiminy Cricket.
$200-$250

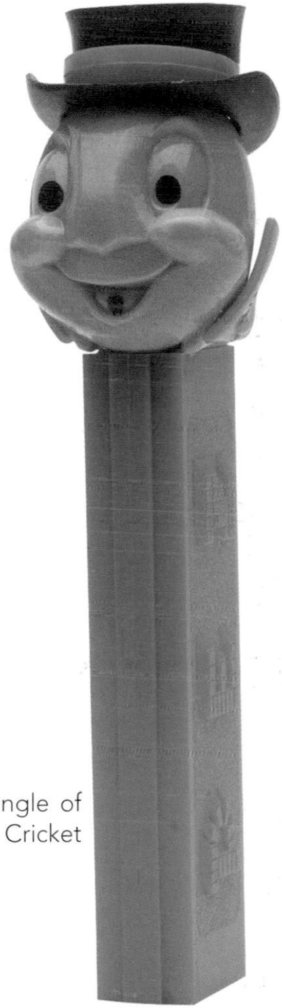

Another angle of the Jiminy Cricket dispenser.

Jungle Book

2003, with feet

European releases of Shere Khan, Bagheera, Mowgli, Baloo, Golden Baloo, and Kaa. Golden Baloo is a European movie promo.

Value:...$3-$4
Golden Baloo:...$10-$15

Jungle Book (L-R): Shere Khan, Bagheera, Mowgli, Baloo, Golden Baloo (**$10-$15**), and Kaa. **$3-$4**
(KP Photo)

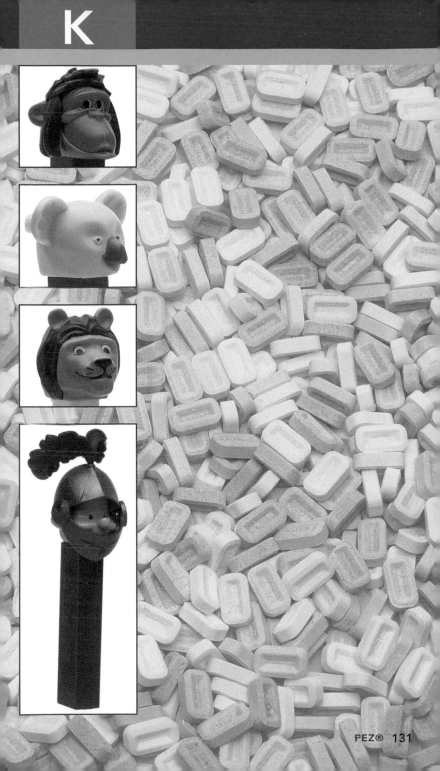

Katrina PEZ®

2005, with feet

Requested by a collector, PEZ® produced a small number as a fund-raising effort to help hurricane victims.

Value: ....$60-$75

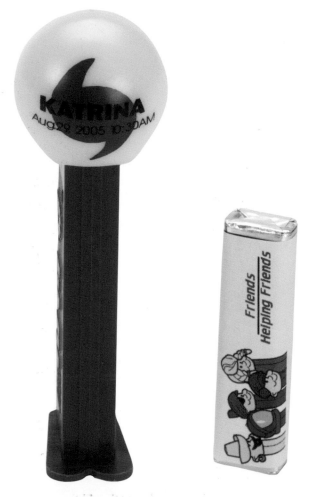

Katrina PEZ®. **$60-$75**
(KP Photo)

King Louie
Late 1960s, no feet and with feet

No feet: ....$30-$45
With feet:...$25-$35
Rare and unusual color variations: ....$300+

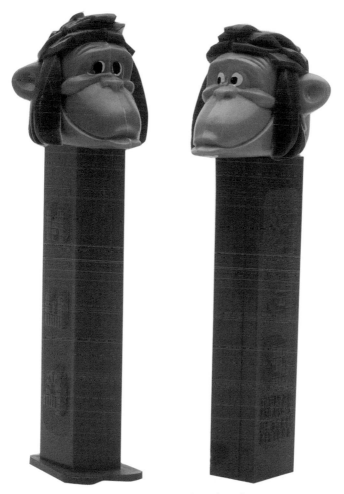

King Louie, (L to R) with feet **$25-$35**, and no feet **$30-$45**.

Knight

Early 1970s, no feet

The Knight was available in three colors—red, black, or white. The white knight is the hardest to find. The plume color on the helmet must always match the stem in order to be correct.

Red: ....$300-$350
Black: ....$350-$375
White: ....$500-$600

Knight with red stem. **$300-$350**, Knight with white stem **$500-$600**, Knight with black stem **$350-$375.**

Koala (whistle)
No feet and with feet

No feet:..$35-$45
With feet: ....$5-$10

Koala whistle with feet. **$5-$10**

Kooky Zoo Crystal Series
2005, with feet
These odd crystal variations were found in "laydown bags" that contained 30 refills and one dispenser.

Value: ....$4-$8

Kooky Zoo Crystal Series. **$4-$8**
(KP Photo)

Kooky Zoo Series

Late 1990s, with feet

Series includes Blinky Bill, a koala and licensed Australian comic character, Lion, Gator, Hippo, and Elephant. A crystal series was available in 1999 through a PEZ® mail-in offer.

A pink elephant and a lion were also released by PEZ® Candy Inc. as part of their "misfits" mail-in offer.

Value: .... **$2-$6 each**
Crystal series: .... **$3-$5 each**
Misfit Elephant and Lion: .... **$3-$5 each**
Zinnafant Elephant: ....**$25-$30**

"Zinnafant" elephant. Done by a European drug company to promote a new antibiotic drug called "Zinnat." Should come with matching candy pack to be considered complete. **$25-$35**

Kooky Zoo series characters, (L to R) Blinky Bill, Lion, Gator, Hippo, and Elephant. **$2-$6**

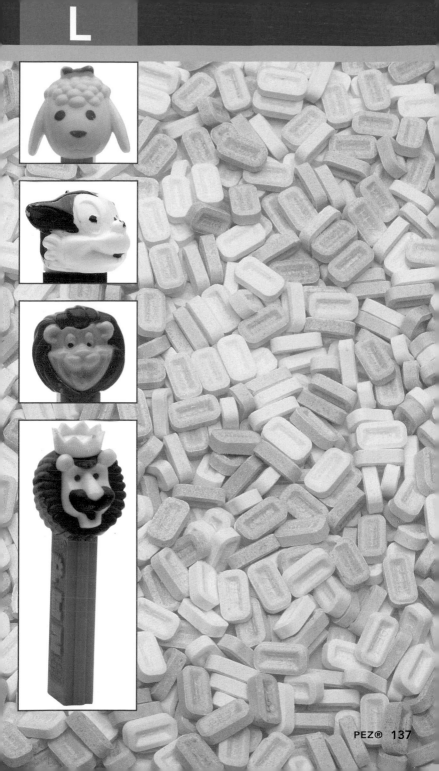

Lamb

1970s, no feet and with feet

No feet: .... $15-$20
With feet: .... $1-$3

Lamb, (L to R) no feet **$15-$20**, with feet. **$1-$3**

Lamb, no feet. **$15-$20**

Lamb (whistle)
No feet and with feet

No feet: .... $25-$35
With feet: .... $15-$25

Lamb, whistle with feet. **$15-$25**

Lil Bad Wolf
Mid-1960s, no feet and with feet

No feet: .... $30-$50
With feet: .... $20-$35

Lil Bad Wolf, no feet. **$30-$50**

Linz Convention
2005, with feet
Commemorated the PEZ® convention in Linz, Austria.

Value: .... $20-$25

2005 Linz PEZ® convention edition. **$20-$25**
(KP Photo)

Lil Lion
Late 1960s, no feet

Value:..$70-$90

Lil Lion. **$70-$90**

Lion King
2004, with feet

Value:...$1-$2

Lion King (L-R): Nala, Timon, Mufasa, Pumbaa, and Simba. **$1-$2 ea**
(KP Photo)

Lion with Crown

Mid-1970s, no feet

This dispenser can be found with several subtle green face color variations and many other different color combinations. The very tough to find red face with white crown goes for twice the price of other variations. Some rare variations can sell for more than double the price.

Value:...$125-$175
Red face/white crown:............................$200-$250

Hard-to-find Lion with Crown variation. **$200-$250**
(From the Johann Patek collection.)

Variations of the Lion with Crown. **$125-$175**
(From the Maryann Kennedy collection.)

Lions Club

1962, no feet

A unique, interesting, and hard-to-find dispenser. Consul Haas was the president of Lions Club, Austria. He commissioned the dispenser for the purpose of handing them out to members who attended the 1962 International Lions Club convention in Nice, France. After the convention, the few pieces of remaining stock had the inscribed stem removed and replaced with a generic PEZ® stem. It was sold in the Circus assortment.

Inscribed stem: .... **$3000+**
Generic stem:... **$2000+**

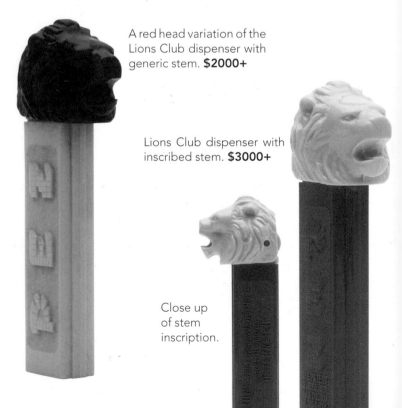

A red head variation of the Lions Club dispenser with generic stem. **$2000+**

Lions Club dispenser with inscribed stem. **$3000+**

Close up of stem inscription.

Looney Tunes Back in Action

2004, with feet
European release

Value:...$3-$5

Looney Tunes Back in Action (L-R): Western Sam, African Taz, French
Tweety, Western Bugs, and Movie Daffy. **$3-$5 each**
(KP Photo)

Looney Tunes Footballs

2006, with feet
European release, in many parts of the world these are called footballs,
but in America they are known as soccer balls.

Value:...$3-$4

Looney Tunes Footballs.
$3-$4 each
(KP Photo)

Magic PEZ®
dispenser

Dispenses candy from the hat and has an additional compartment on the bottom that holds an extra pack of candy that you can make disappear then magically reappear! Can be found in many different color combinations.

Value: .... $3-$6 each

Magic PEZ® dispenser. **$3-$6**

Maharajah

Early 1970s, no feet

There are several variations to this dispenser. One version, made in Hong Kong, has a slightly different turban than the others.

"Hong Kong" version:.... **$100-$125**
Darker green turban: ..... **$120-$140**
Lighter green turban:......... **$75-$90**

A rare black variation.
$NA
(From the Johann Patek collection.)

Maharajah, from the early 1970s. Notice the one on the far left. His turban is shaped slightly different than the other two. This is the "Hong Kong" version **$100-$125**; the one in the middle has a darker green turban **$120-$140**; and the lighter green one on the right is the most common of the three **$75-$90**.

Make-a-Face

Early 1970s, no feet

This dispenser first appeared in 1972, but was quickly discontinued as it had too many tiny pieces that could be easily removed and swallowed by a child. Also, the dispenser was poorly packaged—the bubble frequently came loose from the card, spilling the parts, and rendering it unsaleable. It is rumored what stock was left of these after they were discontinued was ground up, re-melted, and used to mold the headdress for the Indian Chief. The U.S. version contained 17 separate pieces and the European 16, not counting the shoes. This is a very difficult dispenser to find still intact on the card.

U.S. version m.o.c.: .... **$3000+**
European version m.o.c.: .... **$2500+**

A loose Make-a-Face dispenser. **$2500-$3000**

A trio of Make-a-Faces. **$2500-$3000**
(From the Johann Patek collection.)

Front of U.S. card.
(From the Johann Patek collection.)

Back of U.S. card.
(From the Johann Patek collection.)

Front of European card.
(From the Johann Patek collection.)

Back of European card.
(From the Johann Patek collection.)

Madagascar

2005, with feet

Value: ....$1-$2

Madagascar (L-R): Marty the Zebra (two different eye variations), Gloria the Hippo, and Alex the Lion (one version has a painted line under his nose, the other does not). Skipper the penguin is pictured on display boxes but never went into production. **$1-$2**
(KP Photo)

Mary Poppins

Early 1970s, no feet

This dispenser is very difficult to find. As pictured, an even harder to find "painted cheek" variation. One rumor has it this dispenser was in early production when Disney didn't approve the likeness causing PEZ® to halt further distribution, making this a true rarity!

Mary Poppins, with painted cheeks. **$950-$1100**

Value: .... $850-$1000
Painted cheeks: .... $950-$1100

Maximare Elephants

2004 clear, 2005 blue crystal
Maximare Bad Hamm is a European water park.

Value: .... $10-$15

Maximare Elephants. **$10-$**
(KP Photo)

Mexican

Mid-1960s, no feet

With removable hat, goatee, and earrings, this one can be tough to find with all of his pieces.

Value: ....$200-$250

Mexican. **$200-$250**

Additional views of Mexican.

Merlin Mouse

Early 1980s, no feet and with feet

No feet: ....$25-$40
With feet:...........................$12-$15

Merlin Mouse, (L) no feet **$25-$40**, with feet **$12-$15**.

Mickey Mouse

Early 1960s-Present, no feet and with feet
Mickey Mouse has been one of the most popular PEZ® dispensers over the years and has gone through many variations.

Die-cut stem with painted face, early 1960s:......................$300-$400
Die-cut face, early 1960s, no feet: ....$100-$140
Version A, removable nose, early 1970s, no feet:..................$20-$30
Version B, molded nose, early 1980s, no feet:.......................$15-$25
Version B, with feet: ....$10-$15
Version C, stencil eyes, 1990s:...$2-$3
Mickey and Minnie Mouse, current release:..........................$1-$2
Softhead version (rare): ....$3000+

Rare test mold of Mickey Mouse. **$NA**
(From the Johann Patek collection.)

Version B Mickey Mouse no feet (L) **$15-$25**, version C (R) **$2-$3.**

Mickey Mouse with die-cut face pictured (L) **$100-$140**, rare painted version (R) **$NA.**

Mickey and Minnie Mouse, late 1990s edition. **$1-$2**

Rare variations of the painted-face Mickey. **$NA**

(From the Johann Patek collection)

Mickey Mouse version A. **$20-$30**

Mimic the Monkey (Also known as Monkey with Ball Cap)

Mid-1970s, no feet and with feet

Many different head colors were produced, making this an especially fun dispenser to try and collect all variations. Head colors include orange, yellow, red, and blue.

No feet: .... $45-$60
With feet: .... $40-$50

Another color variation of Mimic the Monkey no feet. **$45-$60**

Mimic the Monkey is also known as "Monkey with Ball Cap," no feet. **$45-$60**

Mickey Mouse Extreme

with feet

Value: ....$1-$2

Mickey Mouse Extreme: Pluto, Goofy, Minnie, Mickey, Donald and Daisy. **$1-$2**
(KP Photo)

Monkey (whistle)
No feet and with feet

No feet: ....$40-$60
With feet: ....$25-$30

Monkey, whistle with feet. **$25-$30**

Monkey Sailor
Late 1960s, no feet

The same dispenser was used as Donkey Kong Jr. with one exception, a small transparent sticker was added on his cap with the letter "J." The Donkey Kong Jr. was a 1984 Ralston Purina cereal premium.

Monkey Sailor:...$60-$80
Donkey Kong Jr. with box: ....$100-$500

Side view of Monkey Sailor.

Monkey Sailor. **$60-$80**

Mowgli
Late 1960s, no feet and with feet

No feet: ....$30-$40
With feet:...$25-$35

Mowgli, no feet. **$30-$40**

Mowgli, with feet. **$25-$35**

Mr. Bean

2005, with feet
European release

Value: ....$3-$5 ea

Mr. Bean (L-R): Mr. Bean's car the Mini Cooper,
Mr. Bean, Irma Gobb, and Teddy. **$3-$5**
(KP Photo)

Mr. Mystic

No feet
Some doubt the authenticity of this piece, citing it as
nothing more than the head of Zorro with a ringmaster
hat on it. Currently there is documentation from PEZ®
International that states his existence.

Value: ....$500+

Mr. Mystic. **$500+**
(From the Maryann Kennedy collection.)

Mrs. Clause

2006, with feet
Newest edition to the Christmas series

Value: ....$1-$2

Mrs. Clause. **$1-$2**
(KP Photo)

Mr. Ugly

Early 1970s, no feet and with feet
This really is a homely guy! Several variations to the face coloring exist and differ in value.

Chartreuse green face: ....$75-$95
Aqua green face: ....$80-$90
Olive green face: ....$60-$75
With feet: ....$45-$65

Mr. Ugly with aqua-green faces (L & C) **$** **$90**, and olive green face (R) **$60-$75.**

Mr. Ugly with chartreuse green face. **$75-$95**

Muppets

Early 1990s, with feet

Included in the series are Fozzie Bear, Gonzo, Kermit the Frog, and Miss Piggy. A harder to find version with eyelashes exists of Miss Piggy.

Miss Piggy with eyelashes:..$10-$15
Miss Piggy (common and current versions):...............................$1-$3
Fozzie, Gonzo, and Kermit: ....$1-$2

Miss Piggy (L to R) with eyelashes **$10-$15**, common version **$1-$3**, and current version. **$1-$3.**

Current version of Kermit the Frog. **$1-$2**

Rare Gonzo test mold variation. **$NA**

Kermit, Fozzie Bear, and Gonzo. **$1-$2**

NASCAR

2005-2006, with feet

Helmets (2005), hauler truck sets (2006), and team trucks (2006) have been released so far. With the huge NASCAR following and the fact drivers sometimes change teams, I think the value of these dispensers could rise significantly in the next few years. The 2006-2007 line up will include #24 Jeff Gordon, #17 Matt Kenseth, #5 Kyle Busch, #48 Jimmie Johnson, #99 Carl Edwards, #20 Tony Stewart, #9 Kasey Kahne, #16 Greg Biffle, and #88 Dale Jarrett.

Helmets: ....$1-$2
Hauler Truck Sets: ....$5-$8
Team Trucks: ....$1-$2

NASCAR Helmets (L-R): #17 Matt Kenseth (Dewalt), #2 Rusty Wallace (Miller), #24 Jeff Gordon (DuPont), and #43 Richard Petty (STP). **$1-$2**
(KP Photo)

NASCAR Helmets (L-R): #9 Kasey Kahne, Tony Stewart (Home Depot), and Bobby Labonte (Interstate Batteries). **$1-$2**
(KP Photo)

NASCAR Team Trucks. **$1-$2**
(KP Photo)

NASCAR Hauler Sets: Includes driver's helmet along with the team transport truck packaged as a set. **$5-$8**
(KP Photo)

Nintendo

Late 1990s, with feet

A series not available in the U.S. featuring characters from Nintendo's video games. Dispensers include Diddy Kong, Yoshi, Koopa Trooper, and Mario.

Value: .... **$2-$3 each**

(L to R) Diddy Kong, Yoshi, and Koopa Trooper. **$2-$3**

Mario. **$2-$3**

NCAA College Footballs

2006, with feet

The set will include Georgia Bulldogs, Texas Longhorns, Florida Gators, Alabama Crimson Tide, Florida State Seminoles, Michigan Wolverines, and the Penn State Nittany Lions.

Value: .... **$3-$5 ea**

NCAA College Footballs: Georgia Bulldogs and Texas Longhorns. **$3-$5**
(KP Photo)

NCAA College Footballs: Carded dispenser it also contains the list of all teams.
(KP Photo)

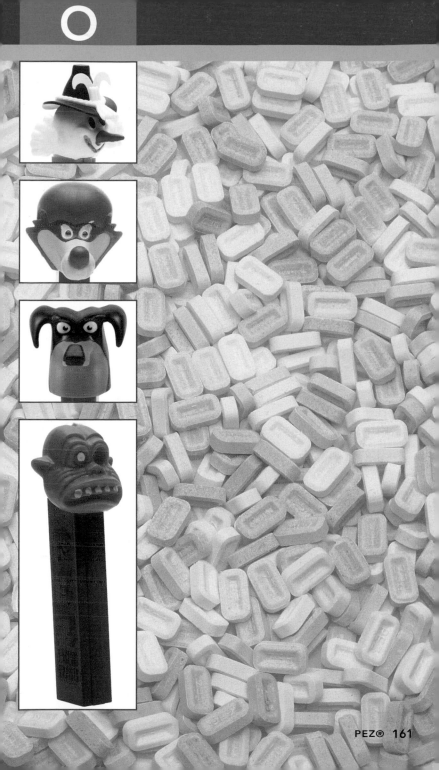

Octopus

Early 1970s, no feet
The Octopus can be found in red, orange, or black.

Orange: ....$85-$95
Black: ....$90-$120
Red: ....$125-$150

Octopus. **$85-$95**

Another Octopus variation. **$85-$95**

Olympic Snowman

No feet
This dispenser was made for the 1976 winter Olympics in Innsbruck, Austria. A very hard-to-find dispenser, it can also be found in a "short nose" version.

Value:..$500-$600

Long-nose version of the Olympic Snowman. **$500-$600**

Olympic Wolves (also called Vucko (voo sh-co) wolves)

With feet

This hard-to-find dispenser was made for the 1984 Olympic games in Sarajevo, Yugoslavia. Variations exist without hat, with hat, and with bobsled helmet.

Wolf, no hat:..$175-$200
Wolf, no hat, unusual brown nose: ....$200-$250
Wolf with hat: ....$225-$275
Wolf with bobsled helmet: ....$250-$300

Vucko with bobsled helmet. **$250-$300**
(From the Maryann Kennedy collection.)

Vucko, without hat. **$175-$200**
(From the Maryann Kennedy collection.)

Vucko shown here with a paper insert.
(From the Maryann Kennedy collection.)

Vucko, with hat (L & C) **$225-$275**, with red bobsled helmet (R) **$250-$300.**

Notice the Olympic rings and Olympic symbol molded into the head.
(From the Maryann Kennedy collection.)

One-Eyed Monster

Early 1970s, no feet and with feet
This dispenser was available with either an orange, brown, gray, pink, or yellow head.

No feet: .... $80-$100
With feet: .... $65-$80

One-eyed Monster, no feet. **$80-$100**

Open Season

2006, with feet
Based on the movie.

Value: ....$1-$2

Open Season (L-R): Elliot (deer), Mr. Weenie (dachshund), Boog (bear), and McSquizzy (beaver). **$1-$2**
(KP Photo)

Orange County Choppers

2006, tin set
Paul Sr., Paul Jr., and Mikey are immortalized as PEZ® dispensers! This set marks the first time PEZ® has placed living people on top of its world-famous candy dispensers—300,000 of these sets were produced and sold out almost immediately.

Value: $15

Orange County Choppers tin set. **$15**
(KP Photo)

Over the Hedge

2006, with feet

Based on the popular motion picture.

Value: .... $1-$2

Over the Hedge (L-R): Stella the skunk, Verne the turtle, RJ the raccoon, and Hammy the squirrel. **$1-$2**
(KP Photo)

Owl (whistle)

With feet

The Owl is very rare and only a few are known to exist.

Value: .... $2000+

Owl whistle. **$2000+**
(From the Maryann Kennedy collection.)

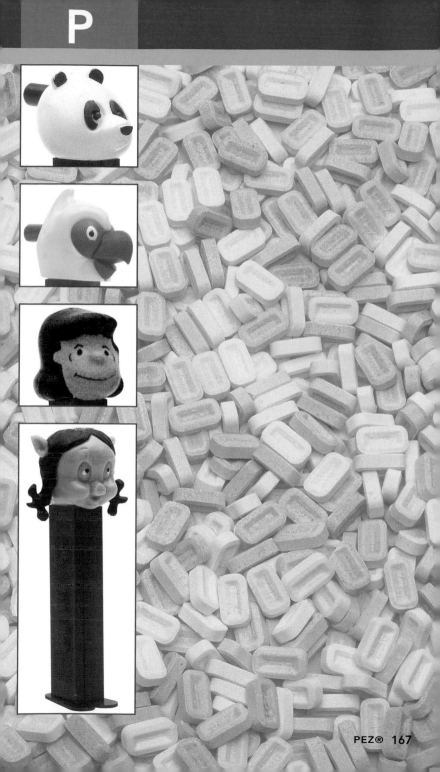

Panda

Early 1970s, no feet and with feet

The Panda has undergone a few modest changes but can still be found today. Rare and hard-to-find colors include the yellow and red head versions.

Removable eyes version (oldest): ....$25-$35
Yellow or red head (with removable eyes):.............. $500+
No feet, stencil eyes:..............$10-$20
Current version:..........................$1-$2

Panda, (L to R) current version **$1-$2**, stencil eyes **$10-$20**, and removable eyes **$25-$35**.

Two rare variations of the Panda— the yellow and red heads. **$500+**
(From the Maryann Kennedy collection.)

Panda (whistle)

No feet and with feet

The Panda was made with removable eyes and with stencil eyes.

Removable eyes, no feet: ....$25-$35
Removable eyes, with feet:...$20-$25
Stencil eyes, with feet:..$5-$10

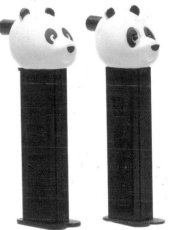

(L to R) Panda whistle with stencil eyes
$5-$10, and removable eyes **$20-$25.**

Panther

Late 1970s, no feet

Value:..$75-$100

Common Panther. **$75-$100**

Parrot (whistle)

No feet and with feet

A rare variation of the Parrot exists with a yellow head and a red beak; more common versions have a red head with a yellow beak.

No feet: ....$15-$20
With feet:...$5-$10
Yellow head, red beak: ....$300+

Parrot whistle with rare yellow head and red beak. **$300+**
(From the Maryann Kennedy collection.)

Party Animals

2007, with feet

Democratic donkey and Republican elephant.

Value: .... $3-$4

Party Animals. **$3-$4**
(KP Photo)

Peanuts

Early 1990s to current, with feet
Characters include Charlie Brown, Lucy, Snoopy, Woodstock, and Peppermint Patty. Several variations exist for each.

Charlie Brown, smiling: ....$1-$2
Charlie Brown, frowning (non-U.S.): ....$5-$10
Charlie Brown, tongue showing (non-U.S.): ....$5-$10
Charlie Brown, eyes closed (non-U.S.):....................................$50-$60
Lucy, common version:...$1-$2
Lucy, white around eyes:...$50-$75
Lucy, white face (known as "psycho Lucy"): ....$75-$90
Peppermint Patty:..$1-$2
Snoopy:...$1-$3
Snoopy as "Joe Cool":...$1-$3
Woodstock, common version:..$1-$2
Woodstock with feathers
(black markings on the top and back of his head):....................$3-$5

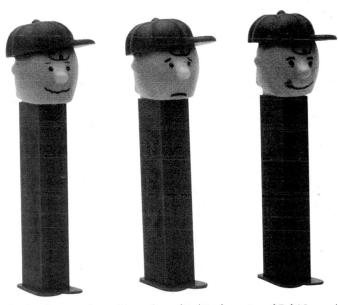

Charlie Brown, (L to R) smiling **$1-$2**, frowning **$5-$10**, and with tongue showing **$5-$10.**

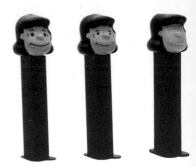

Lucy, (L to R) common version **$1-$2**, white around eyes **$50-$75**, and white face (Psycho Lucy) **$75-$90**.

Peppermint Patty, **$1-$2**, and Joe Cool **$1-$3**.

Woodstock, common version (L) **$1-$2**, Woodstock with feathers (C) **$3-$5**, and Snoopy **$1-$3**.

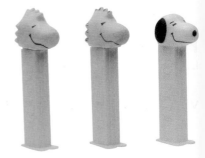

Peanuts 2000. Charlie Brown **$1-$2**, Lucy **$1-$2**, Snoopy **$1-$3**, and Woodstock **$1-$2**.

Penguin (whistle)

With feet

Value:...$5-$10

Penguin, whistle. **$5-$10**

Peter Pan

Late 1960s, no feet

Value:...$175-$225

Peter Pan. **$175-$225**

Peter PEZ®

Late 1970s, no feet and with feet
A dispenser featuring the clown mascot of the PEZ® Candy company. The original was produced in the late 1970s and a remake came out in the early 1990s.

Original version, no feet: ....$75-$100
Remake (1993 to 2001):............$2-$4
Current: ....$1-$2
"Rico" variation:....................$20-$30

Peter PEZ® "Rico" variation. "Rico" means candy. **$20-$30**

2001 version of Peter PEZ®, (L) **$2-$4,** mail-order variation dispenser glows in the dark **$5-$10.**

Petunia Pig

Early 1980s, no feet and with feet

No feet: ....$40-$50
With feet: ....$30-$40

Petunia Pig, with feet. **$30-$40**

PEZ® Writing Pen

Sometimes called the "Robot PEZ," its actually the inside, candy dispensing portion of the PEZ® Writing Pen. Some collectors dismantle the pen to get to this dispenser then sell it as a "Robot PEZ," while others have listed it on eBay as a rare dispenser actually made by PEZ®. These can be neat for display, but serve as a perfect example of a collectible that can be misleading—always know what you are buying, especially before spending a lot of money.

Value: ....$1-$2

Inside of PEZ® Writing Pen. **$1-$2**
(KP Photo)

PEZ® Convention Dispensers

2002-2006, with feet

A premium for registered guests of annual PEZ® collector conventions. The first dispenser in 2002 was a witch, and the initial shipment was meant to be part of the Halloween holiday assortment, but it arrived from the manufacturer with the wrong colors. PEZ® graciously donated the "misfits" to each of the collector convention hosts to distribute among registered guests. Its success prompted PEZ® to offer convention premiums in following years.

2002, **Glow in the Dark Witch:** ....$20-$30

2003, **Crystal Head Snowman:** ....$20-$30

2004, **Crystal Head Bee:** ....$20-$30

2004, **Crystal Globe:** ....$25-$35 (Linz convention in Austria)

2005, **Chick in Egg:** ....$20-$30

2006, **No convention dispenser was produced.**

The PEZ® Convention Dispensers.
(KP Photo)

Philadelphia Kixx

2002, with feet

This soccer ball is another in the growing line of sports-related dispensers.

Value:..$25-$30

Philadelphia Kixx. **$25-$30**
(KP Photo)

PIF the Dog

With feet

PIF was offered as a premium in a German "YPS" comic in 1989. If you look closely you can see his name PIF on his left ear.

Value: ....$85-$100

PIF the Dog. **$85-$100**

Pig (whistle)
No feet and with feet

No feet: .... $50-$60
With feet:.. $35-$45

Pig, with feet. **$35-$45**

Pilgrim
Mid-1970s, no feet
The Pilgrim can be found with either a white or yellow hatband.

Value: .... **$150-$175**

Pilgrim. **$150-$175**

Pilot and Stewardess
Mid-1970s, no feet

Pilot: .... $175-$200
Stewardess: .... $150-$175

Stewardess. **$150-$175**

Pilot. **$175-$200**

Pink Panther

Late 1990s, with feet

Not available in the U.S., this series featured the Pink Panther, Inspector Clousseau, Ant, and Aardvark.

Value:.. $2-$3 each
2002 "Pinky" remake:.............................$5-$10

2002 "Pinky" version
of the Pink Panther.
$5-$10

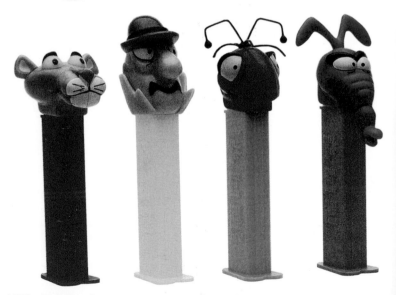

1990s Pink Panther series (L to R) Pink Panther, Inspector Clouseau, Ant, and Aardvark. **$2-$3**

Pinocchio

Early 1960s, no feet

Two versions of Pinocchio were made—one in the early 1960s and the other in the early 1970s. The earlier version (A) can be found with either a red or yellow hat.

Version A: ....$175-$225
Version B:..$140-$165

Pinocchio, A version. **$175-$225**

Pirate

Early 1970s, no feet
Variations can be found in the Pirate's bandana and in his skin tone.

Value: .... **$75-$100**

Pirate. **$75-$100**

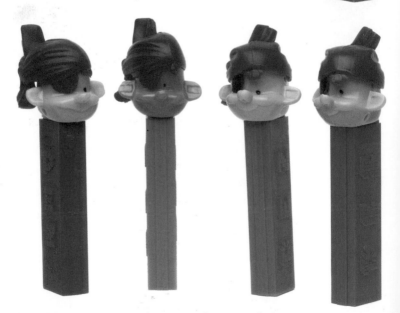

More Pirate variations. The unusual orange-flesh variation is pictured second from left. **$75-$100**

Playworld Sets

Early 1990s, with feet, Non-U.S.
These sets featured a single dispenser along with a matching body part. The sets usually have a theme such as Easter or Christmas. The cardboard piece inserted in the package unfolded into three sections. It contained related scenery that could serve as a backdrop in which to play with the dispenser.

Easter set:...$20-$25
Christmas set: ....$3-$5
Shell Gas set: ....$20-$25

Easter Playworld set. **$20-$25**

Christmas Playworld set. **$3-$5**

Shell Gas Playworld set. **$20-$25**

Pluto

Early 1960s to current, no feet and with feet
Several versions of Pluto, Mickey Mouse's faithful dog, have been produced through the years.

Version A, round head and movable ears, no feet: ....$25-$30
Version A, "Hong Kong": ....$20-$25
Version B, flat head and movable ears: ....$10-$15
Version C, molded ears: ....$2-$5
Version D, (current): ....$1-$2

Pluto, the two on the left are version B and are sometimes called the flathead version **$10-$15**, version C is second from right **$2-$5**, and the far right is version D **$1-$2**.

Pluto, first appeared in the early 1960s. (L to R) Original "Hong Kong" version **$20-$25**, original version **$25-$30**, and caramel variation of original version **$25-$30**.

Pokémon

2001, with feet

Value: ....$2-$4

Pikachu. **$2-$4**

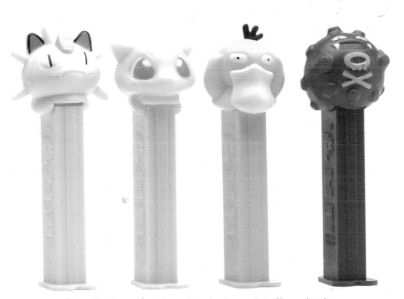

(L to R) Meowth, Mew, Psyduck, and Koffing. **$2-$4**

Policeman
Early 1970s, no feet

Value:..$50-$75

Policeman. **$50-$75**

Political Elephant

No feet

This is an extremely rare dispenser, only a few are known to exist. It is thought to represent the elephant of the Republican political party. In early 1997 an old file was discovered in the PEZ® factory in Connecticut containing a press release and an old photo of a special set of dispensers. The press release was dated June 13, 1961 and had the heading "President Kennedy receives PEZ® souvenirs on his visit to Vienna." It went on to detail the set and then said "To the President of the United States of America J.F. Kennedy with the Compliments of PEZ®." The set contained in a wooden, cigar-like box had three dispensers; a Donkey for the President (to represent the Democratic Party), a Golden Glow for Jackie, a Bozo die-cut for Caroline, and three packs of candy for each. To date, this set has yet to surface. The elephant as pictured has a shiny, golden-colored head with his trunk extending over the top of his head.

Value: .... $8000+

Very rare variation of the Political Elephant. **$8000+**
(From the Johann Patek collection.)

Another rare variation of the Political Elephant. **$8000+**
(From the Johann Patek collection.)

Pony (also known as Pony-Go-Round)

Early 1970s, no feet

This dispenser can be found in MANY different colors and it's fun to search for variations. Some are very difficult to find such as the green, pink, and purple heads and these versions can bring up to five times as much as the more common color combinations.

Value (common color combinations): .... $100-$150

Pony, also known as the Pony-Go-Round, can be found in many different colors. The green, pink, and purple heads are less common variations and can bring up to five times as much as more common color variations.

(From the Maryann Kennedy collection.)

Pony. **$100-$150**
(From the Maryann Kennedy collection.)

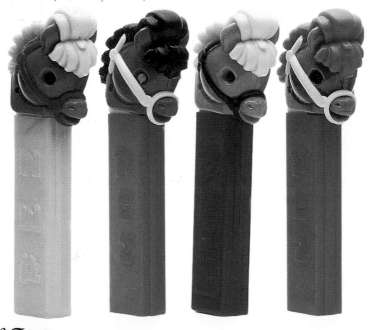

Popeye

Late 1950s to late 1970s, no feet
Some believe Popeye was the first licensed character PEZ® ever used on a dispenser. Brutus and Olive Oyl were produced in the mid-1960s and usually are found with missing or chipped paint on their faces.

Popeye, original version, hat is molded to the head: ....$150-$175
Popeye B, plain face: ....$125-$150
Popeye C, with pipe (note the pipe is the same piece used on
Mickey Mouse's nose): ....$100-$125
Brutus: ....$250-$275
Olive Oyl: ....$275-$325

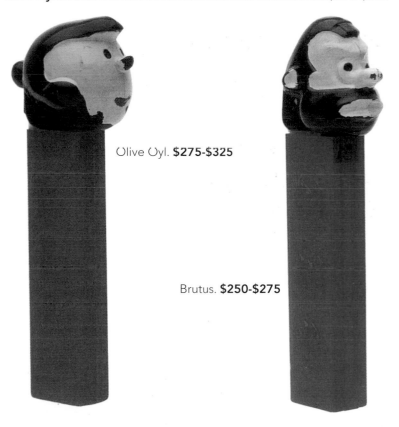

Olive Oyl. **$275-$325**

Brutus. **$250-$275**

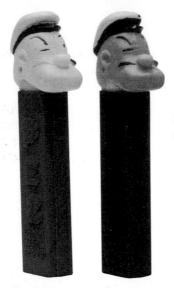

Popeye, original version with hat molded to head. **$150-$175**

Popeye, version B (L) **$125-$150**, version B with removable pipe (C & R) **$100-$125.**

Practical Pig

1960s, no feet and with feet

Two versions were produced—the earlier version (version A) has a flat hat and the later version (B) produced in the 1970s, has a wavy hat.

Version A, no feet: ....$40-$60
Version A, with feet: ....$25-$35
Version B, no feet: ....$60-$75
Version B, with feet: ....$30-$40

Practical Pig, version A with feet (L) **$25-$35**, and no feet (R) **$40-$60**.

Practical Pig, version B with feet (l) **$30-$40, and no feet (R)** **$60-$75.**

Psychedelic Flower

Late 1960s, no feet

Very much a product of their time, these dispensers came packaged with flower flavor candy. They can be found with several different stickers

including, "mod pez," "go-go pez," and different "luv pez" versions on at least one side. The side that has the sticker will be completely smooth. Some dispensers had stickers on both sides and are considered to be worth a bit more than a one-sticker dispenser.

A collector's edition remake was produced in the late 1990s and was available from PEZ® through a mail-in offer. The remake versions have the raised PEZ® logo on the stem and do not have stickers on either side. They are also marked with a copyright symbol and 1967—the originals do not have a date on them.

Original:......................................$350-$450
Remake, m.o.c.: ....$5-$10

Original Psychedelic Flower.
$350-$450

Comparison of a vintage Psychedelic Flower (L) and a remake (R).

Hard–to-find yellow and deep red flower variations. **$NA**

Psychedelic Hand

Late 1960s, no feet

The Hand also came packaged with flower flavor candy, and will have at least one sticker. The side that has the sticker will be completely smooth. Some dispensers had stickers on both sides and are considered to be worth a bit more than a one-sticker dispenser.

A collector's edition remake was produced in the late 1990s and was only available through a PEZ® mail-in offer. The remake versions have the raised PEZ® logo on the stem and do not have stickers on either side. They are also marked with a copyright symbol and 1967—the originals do not have a date on them.

Original: ....$300-$400
Original, black hand:...$450-$550
Remake, m.o.c.: ....$5-$10

Original black Psychedelic Hand variation. **$450-$550**

Original Psychedelic Hand dispensers. **$300-$400**

Silver and gold remakes. **$30-$50 ea** (KP Photo)

Comparison of the original dispenser (L) and the remake (R).

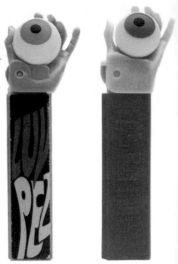

Collector's Edition Hand on card—offered by PEZ® in 1998 through a mail-in offer. **$5-$10**

A grouping of original Psychedelic Hands. **$300-$400**

A grouping of black Psychedelic hands. **$450-$550**

Raven

Early 1970s, no feet and with feet

Two versions were made of the Raven—one with a short beak and one with a long beak. The beak can be found in either yellow or red. The long beak was not released in the U.S. and usually sells for about twice that of the regular version.

Short beak, no feet: ....$75-$90
Short beak, feet: ....$50-$75
Long beak: ....$150-$200

Red short beak with feet version of Raven (L) **$50-$75**, and long beak version (R) **$150-$200**.
(Long beak from the Maryann Kennedy collection.)

Yellow short beak no feet version of Raven. **$75-$90**

Yellow long beak version of Raven. **$150-$200**
(Long beak from the Maryann Kennedy collection.)

Regular, Advertising

These dispensers were never mass-produced. Most were screened one at a time and in very small quantities. They were given to customers and sales reps as "business cards." Ad Regulars are very difficult to find, and from time to time previously unknown ads turn up. The ultra-rare "Lonicot" regular is among the rarest of the Advertising dispensers. Only two are currently known to exist. Lonicot is German for "low nicotine." PEZ® was touted as an alternative to smoking, so for a brief time they experimented with a candy that actually contained nicotine. This is the container that was to dispense that candy. To this date no candy has been found, only the dispenser and a small bit of paperwork.

Value: .... $1000-$1500 each
Lonicot dispenser: .... $6000+

Safeway ad regular.
$1000-$1500
(From the Johann Patek collection.)

The ultra-rare "Lonicot" regular. **$6000+**
(From the Maryann Kennedy collection.)

Bosch ad regulars. **$1000-$1500**
(From the Johann Patek collection.)

Regular, Box Patent

Early 1950s

This is believed to be the second-generation dispenser design, the box trademark being the first. It was not sold in the U.S. and is a very rare dispenser.

Value: .... **$2000+**

Box Patent regular (non U.S.). A very rare dispenser. **$2000+**
(From the Maryann Kennedy collection.)

Regular, Box Trademark

Late 1940s to early 1950s

Thought to be the first generation of dispenser design.

Value: .... $3000+

Box Trademark regular. **$3000+**
(From the Johann Patek collection.)

Regular, Locking Cap

Late 1940s

Value:.. $2500+

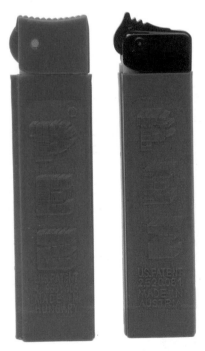

Comparison of a new regular (L), and a vintage regular (R).

Rare Locking Cap regular. **$2500+**
(From the Johann Patek collection.)

Regular, New
Mid-1990s

A new line of Regulars were produced in the 1990s, but with a noticeable difference in the cap. There was also a new line of Regulars with different colors available only in Japan.

New U.S. regulars: ....$3-$5
New Japan regulars
Pink, white, or gray:...$5-$10
Gold:...$30-$40
Black: ....$15-$20

Rare long gray regular and "Klick and Spend" ad regular. **$NA**
(From the Johann Patek collection.)

Newer regulars with matching inner sleeves. These are known as "mono regulars." **$NA**
(From the Johann Patek collection.)

Current line of U.S. regulars. **$3-$5**

More color variations of the current line of U.S. regulars. **$3-$5**

Regular, Original

Here it is, the ORIGINAL PEZ® regular! This little guy is just over 3/4-inch wide and barely measures 2-1/2-inches tall. It matches the size of the mechanical drawing for patent number 2,620,061 exactly!

The only known original PEZ® regular. **$NA**
(From the Johann Patek collection.)

The opposite side.

With the sleeve extended.

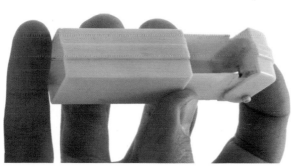

Regular, Vintage

1950s

There are many different cap/stem color combinations including some that are semi-transparent through which you can see the inner workings of the dispenser.

Value: ....**$100-$150**

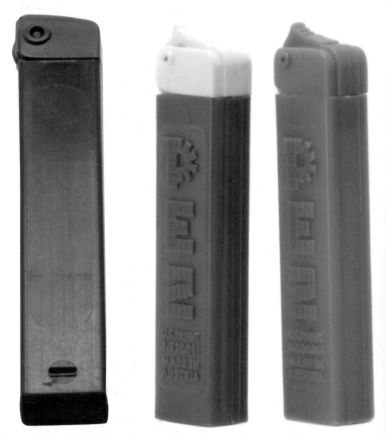

Disposable vintage regular. **$100-$150**

Vintage regulars. **$100-$150**
(From the Johann Patek collection.)

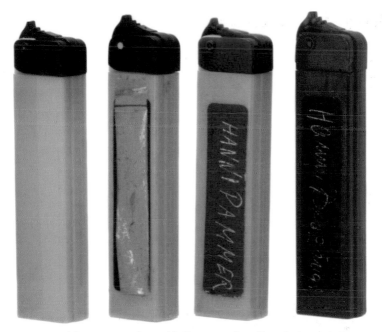

Vintage regulars with "personalized" variations.
(From the Johann Patek collection.)

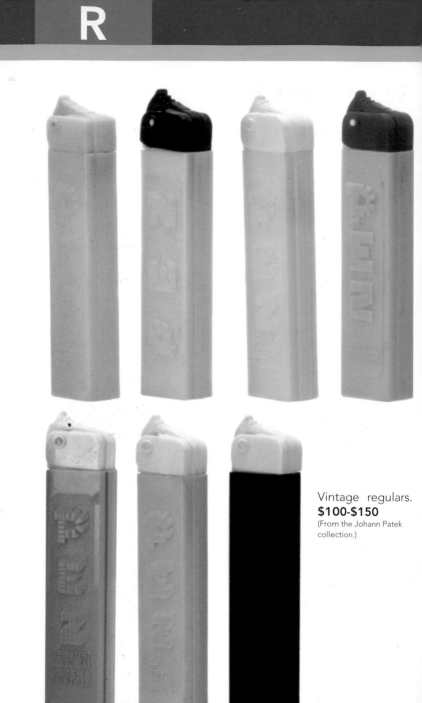

Vintage regulars.
$100-$150
(From the Johann Patek collection.)

Regular, Witch

Mid-1950s

This is among the rarest of PEZ® dispensers. A picture of a witch is screened on both sides of the stem.

Value: .... $3500+

Dark orange Witch
regular. **$3500+**
(From the Johann Patek collection.)

Light orange Witch
regular. **$3500+**
(From the Johann Patek collection.)

Rhino (whistle)
No feet and with feet

No feet: ....$15-$25
With feet:..$5-$10

Rhino, whistle with feet. **$5-$10**

Ringmaster
Mid-1970s, no feet
An uncommon dispenser—and usually found missing his moustache.

Value: .... $275-$350

Ringmaster. **$275-$350**

Roadrunner

Early 1980s, no feet and with feet

Painted eyes, no feet: ....$30-$40
Painted eyes, with feet: ....$25-$30
Stencil eyes, with feet (this is the most common version):.....$20-$25

Roadrunner, stencil eyes with feet. **$20-$25**, painted eyes with feet **$25-$30**, and painted eyes no feet **$30-$40**.

Robot (Also known as the Spacetrooper)

1950s

This is one of the few "full body" dispensers. They stand approximately 3-1/2" tall and have the letters "PEZ" on their back. They are tough to find.

Red: .... $250-$300
Yellow: .... $300-$350
Blue: .... $275-$300
Dark blue: .... $300-$400
Shiny gold (very rare): ... $2000+

Very rare gold robot. **$2000+**
(From the Johann Patek collection.)

Robot, red. **$250-$300**

Robot, blue (L) **$275-$300**, and dark blue (R) **$300-$400**.

Robot, yellow. **$300-$350**

Rooster

Mid-1970s, no feet

There are several different color variations with white being the most common followed by yellow and green.

White: ....$40-$50
Yellow or green:..$65-$85

Rooster, green head. **$65-$85**
(From the Maryann Kennedy collection.)

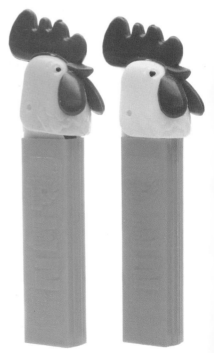

Rooster, yellow head (L) **$65-$85**, and white head **$40-$50**.

Rooster (whistle)

No feet and with feet

No feet: ....$35-$45
With feet:...$25-$35

Rooster, whistle with feet. **$25-$35**

Rudolph

Late 1970s, no feet and with feet
The mold used to produce Bambi was also used for Rudolph—but the nose on Rudolph was painted red.

No feet: ....$50-$75
With feet:...$35-$50

Rudolph, no feet. **$50-$75**

Sailor

Late 1960s, no feet

Value: ....**$175-$225**

Sailor. **$175-$225**

Santa

1950s to Present, no feet and with feet

Santa is one of the most popular PEZ® dispensers ever produced. Most commonly found is Santa C, which has been produced since the 1970s.

Santa A, no feet, face and beard are the same color: ....**$120-$150**
Santa B, no feet, flesh-colored face with white beard: ......**$125-$160**
Santa C, no feet: ....**$5-$10**
Santa C, with loop for ornament:..**$35-$50**
Santa C, with feet: ....**$2-$3**
Santa D, with feet:..**$1-$2**
Santa E, (current): ....**$1-$2**
Full body Santa (1950s): ....**$150-$200**

Santa, version A (L) **$120-$150**, B version (R) **$125-$160**.

Full Body Santa. **$150-$200**

Santa, version C with feet **$2-$3**, and
version D **$1-$2**.

Scrooge McDuck

Late 1970s, no feet and with feet

The original version used the same mold that was used for Donald Duck version B, with the glasses, sideburns, and hat as separately molded pieces (and easily lost). The remake version has molded sideburns.

Original, no feet: ....$30-$40
Original, with feet:...$25-$35
Remake version:..$5-$10

Scrooge McDuck, original no feet **$30-$40**, remake version. **$5-$10**

Sesame Street

2005, with feet

In addition to offering Cookie Monster, Zoe, Bert, Ernie, Elmo, and Big Bird, PEZ® also offered collector's versions of Big Bird, Elmo, and Cookie Monster on their Web site that came packaged in special boxes celebrating the 25th anniversary of Sesame Street.

2005 releases:.. $1-$2 each
25th anniversary editions:.............................. $15-$20 each

Sesame Street (L-R): Cookie Monster, Zoe, Bert, Ernie, Elmo and Big Bird.
$1-$2
(KP Photo)

Sheik

Early 1970s, no feet

The Sheik can be found with either a red or black band on top of the burnoose.

Red band: ....$90-$125
Black band: ....$125-$150

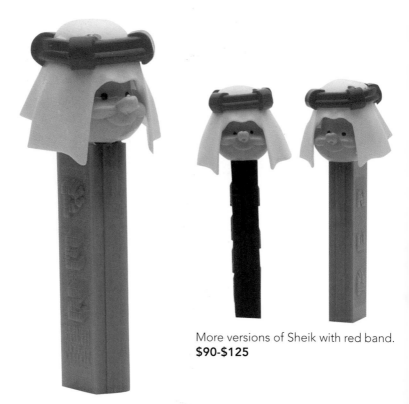

More versions of Sheik with red band.
$90-$125

Sheik, red band. **$90-$125**

Sheriff

Late 1970s, no feet

Value: ....$150-$200

Sheriff. **$150-$200**

Shrek 2

2004 European release, with feet
The silver donkey was done as a European movie promo.

Value: ....$2-$4
Silver Donkey: ....$5-$10

Shrek 2 (L-R): Shrek, Ogress Fiona, Puss 'n Boots, and Donkey. **$2-$4**
(KP Photo)

Silver Glow

1991
These were made to commemorate the opening of a new plant in Hungary.

Carded: .... $25-$40
Loose: .... $15-$25

Silver Glow. **$15-$25**

Simpsons

Spring 2000, with feet
Doh! It's the whole Simpson family! Marge, Homer,
Bart, Lisa, and Maggie.

Value: .... **$1-$2 each**

Bart Simpson. **$1-$2**

Maggie, Lisa, Homer, and Marge Simpson. **$1-$2**

Skull

Early 1970s to current, no feet and with feet

A "misfit" version of the skull with a black head was available in 1998 through a mail-in offer. A very hard-to-find variation of version B is known as the "Colgate" skull, because he has a full set of teeth!

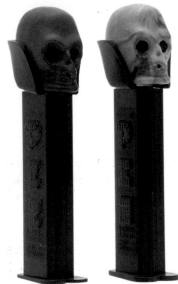

Version A, no feet: ....$15-$20
Version A, with feet:.............$10-$15
Version B, larger head: ....$1-$3
Version B, glows in the dark:....$1-$3
"Misfit" version: ....$5-$8
Full set of teeth: ....$50-$60

Rare marbleized Skull variations.
$NA
(From the Johann Patek collection.)

Skull, (L to R) version A no feet **$15-$20**, version A with feet **$10-$15**, version B with larger head **$1-$3**, and Misfit version **$5-$8**.

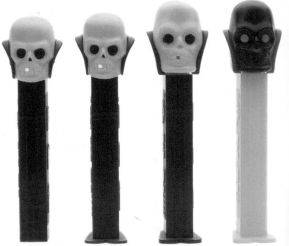

Smiley

Have a nice day! It's the smiley face dispenser, this guy can be found on purple, green, orange, blue, or yellow stems.

Value: .... **$1-$3**

Smiley. **$1-$3**

Smurfs

Late 1980s, no feet and with feet

Two Smurf series were produced—one in the late 1980s and the second in the late 1990s. Series one included Smurf, Smurfette, and Papa Smurf. The second series includes Smurf, Papa Smurf, Smurfette, Brainy Smurf, and Gargamel.

Smurf (first series): ....**$10-$15**
Smurfette (first series): ....**$10-$15**
Papa Smurf (first series): ....**$10-$15**
Second series: .... **$3-$5 each**

Brainy Smurf and Gargamel, second series. **$3-$5**

Smurfs, original series, including Smurf, Papa Smurf, and Smurfette with feet **$5-$10**, and no feet **$10-$15**.

Second series Smurf, Papa Smurf, and Smurfette. **$3-$5**

Snow White

Late 1960s, no feet
Collar color variations include white, yellow, turquoise, and green.
Turquoise is worth slightly more.

Value: ....$200-$225

Snow White. **$200-$225**
(From the Maryann Kennedy collection.)

Additional color variations of Snow
White. **$200-$225**

Snowman
1970s, no feet and with feet

No feet: .... $15-$25
With feet:................................... $1-$5
**"Misfit" versions
(mail-in offer, late 1990s):** .... $5-$8

Snowman, "misfit" versions. **$5-$8**

Snowman, no feet **$15-$25**, and with feet **$1-$5**.

Softhead Superheroes

Late 1970s, no feet

The heads on these dispensers are made of a soft eraser-like material and usually found only on USA marked stems. These are very popular with collectors. Characters in the series include: Batman, Penguin, Wonder Woman, Joker, and Batgirl.

Value: .... **$150-$200 each**

Batman Softhead Superhero. **$150-$200**

Penguin and Wonder Woman Softhead Superheroes. **$150-$200**

Joker and Batgirl Softhead Superheroes. **$150-$200**

Sourz

Released summer of 2002. Pineapple, blue raspberry, watermelon, and green apple come with new sour PEZ® candy!

Colored Crystal Sourz: .... **$4-$6 each**
Clear Crystal Sourz: .... **$4-$6 each**

Sourz
Pineapple.
$1-$2

Sourz Blue Raspberry, Watermelon, and Green Apple. **$1-$2**

Colored Crystal Sourz (2005): Sour Green Apple, Sour Blue Raspberry, Sour Pineapple, and Sour Watermelon. This colored crystal set along with the clear crystal version were originally sold as mail order items from Pez.com. In the fall of 2005 PEZ® decided to package the remaining inventory and sell it at a discount to a dollar type retailer on the West coast. This move significantly dropped the value of the sets and angered many collectors. **$4-$6 ea**
(KP Photo)

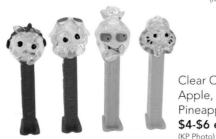

Clear Crystal Sourz (2005): Sour Green Apple, Sour Blue Raspberry, Sour Pineapple and Sour Watermelon. **$4-$6 ea**
(KP Photo)

Spaceman

Late 1950s, no feet

A premium version of the Spaceman was offered by Cocoa Marsh in the late 1950s. The premium version had "Cocoa Marsh" on the stem. Several stem variations include light blue, dark blue, and metallic blue, as well as clear or transparent blue helmet.

Value: .... $150-$175
Cocoa Marsh Spaceman: .... $175-$225

Cocoa Marsh Spaceman. **$175-$225**

Spaceman dispenser, from the late 1950s. Same as Cocoa Marsh Spaceman, except this one has the PEZ® logo on both sides **$150-$175**.

Sparefroh

Early 1970s, no feet

"Sparefroh" is German for "happy saver." October 31st of each year in Europe is World Savings Day when all people are encouraged to save money in a bank. (Thus the tie-in with the coin that is glued to the front of the stem.) This was a gift to children who put money in their bank account on that day. There are two different stem inscriptions: "110 Jahre Allgemeine Sparkasse in Linz" and "Deine Sparkasse." The coin must be attached to the dispenser to be considered complete.

Value: ....**$1200-$1500**

Sparefroh. **$1200-$1500**

Speedy Gonzales
Late 1970s to current, no feet and with feet

No feet: ....$30-$40
With feet, older head:..$15-$25
Current: ....$1-$2

Speedy Gonzales, current version. **$1-$2**

Spider-Man

Late 1970s, no feet and with feet
Several versions of Spider-Man have been produced.

Smaller head, no feet:..$15-$20
Medium size head, with feet:................................$5-$8
Larger head, with feet (current): ....$1-$2

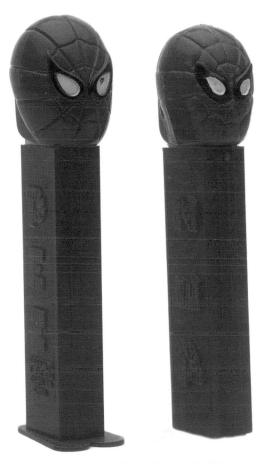

Spider-Man, Late 1970s with feet **$5-$8**, and no feet **$15-$20**.

Spike

Early 1980s, no feet and with feet

Spike was not released in the U.S. Several versions exist including small painted eyes, decal eyes and an unusual variation with a green head.

Decal eyes:..$5-$10
Small painted eyes:...$15-$20
Green head: ....$100-$125

Spike, decal eyes. **$5-$10**

Spike, small painted eyes. **$15-$20**

Sponge Bob Square Pants
2004, with feet

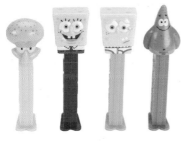

Value:......................................$1-$2

Sponge Bob (L-R): Squidward, Sponge Bob, Embarrassed Sponge Bob, and Patrick. **$1-$2**
(KP Photo)

Sportz Pez
2004, with feet
Mail-order items from Pez.com

Value:..................$10-$15 set

LSU football (2004) **$25-$30**; Metro Stars hockey puck (2004) **$15-$20**; and Golden Football (2005) **$10-$15**.
(KP Photo)

Baseball, Football, Basketball, and Hockey Puck. **$10-$15 set**
(KP Photo)

Star Wars

Late 1990s-current, with feet

PEZ® released four series of dispensers featuring characters from the *Star Wars* universe. The first series included five dispensers: Darth Vader, Stormtrooper, C3-PO, Yoda, and Chewbacca. The second series, released summer of 1999 included: Ewok, Princess Leia, Boba Fett, and Luke Skywalker. The third series released summer 2002 in conjunction with the movie *Attack of the Clones* featured Jango Fett, R2-D2, and Clone Trooper. The fourth series released summer of 2005 included Chewbacca, Death Star, Emperor Palpatine (regular version), Emperor Palpatine (Wal-Mart glow-in-the-dark version), and General Grievous.

The 2005 collectors edition box set was limited to 250,000 sets and included nine dispensers: Death Star, Boba Fett, General Grievous, Emperor Palpatine, Darth Vader, R2-D2, Chewbacca, Yoda, and C3-PO.

Value (all series): .... **$1-$3 each**
Emperor Palpatine glow-in-the-dark: ....**$3-$5**
2005 boxed set:..**$20-$25**
2005 boxed set with glow-in-the-dark Emperor Palpatine: ...**$25-$30**

Jango Fett. **$1-$3**

R2-D2 and Clone Trooper. **$1-$3**

Emperor Palpatine (Wal-Mart glow in the dark version). **$3-$5**

(L-R): Chewbacca, Death Star, Emperor Palpatine (regular version), and General Grievous. **$1-$2**

Sylvester

Late 1970s, no feet and with feet
Several versions of Tweety Bird's nemesis exist.

No feet: ....$15-$20
With feet, older style head: ....$5-$8
With feet, with whiskers
(black lines under nose), non-U.S. version:....................$4-$8
Current: ....$1-$2

Sylvester, two variations of current version. **$1-$2**

Sylvester, no feet **$15-$20**, with feet and older-style head **$5-$8**, and with feet and whiskers **$4-$8**.

Swedish Soccer Ball

2004, with feet
The left side of this dispenser's unique card contains a photo of the entire team.

Loose:..$20-$25
MOC: ....$25-$30

Swedish Soccer Ball.
(KP Photo)

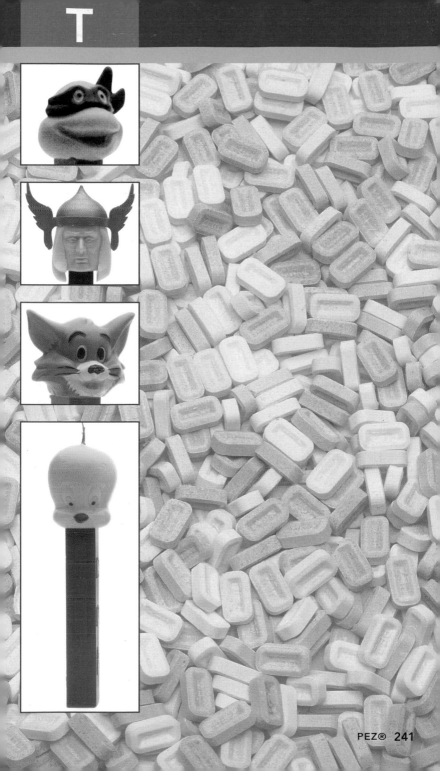

Tazmanian Devil

Late 1990s, with feet

Value:..$1-$2
Cycling Taz (with hat): ....$1-$2

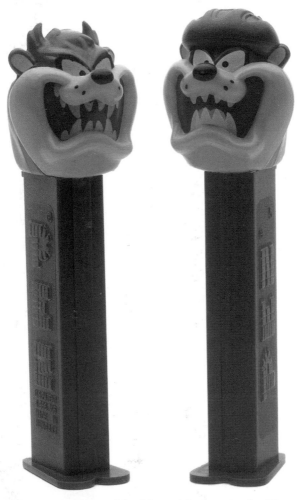

Tazmanian Devil **$1-$2**, and Cycling Taz **$1-$2**.

Teenage Mutant Ninja Turtles

Mid-1990s, with feet

Two series were produced—a smiling version and an angry version of Leonardo, Michaelangelo, Donatello, and Raphael. With 8 different turtle heads and 8 stem colors, collecting all variations presents a bit of a challenge.

Smiling version:......................$2-$3 each
Angry version:........................$2-$3 each
2005 Remakes: ....$1-$2 each

Teenage Mutant Ninja Turtles, Leonardo smiling version. **$2-$3**

Teenage Mutant Ninja Turtles, angry version Leonardo, Raphael, Donatello, and Michaelangelo. **$2-$3**

Teenage Mutant Ninja Turtles 2005 remakes (L-R): Raphael, Michelangelo, Leonardo, and Donatello. **$1-$2**
(KP Photo)

Thor
Late 1970s, no feet

Value: .... $250-$300

Thor. **$250-$300**

Thumper
Late 1970s, no feet and with feet
A very subtle yet pricey variation of this dispenser has the copyright symbol along with the letters "WDP" on the head.

No feet, no copyright: ....$85-$100
With feet: ....$60-$80
With copyright: .... $200+

Thumper, with feet. **$60-$80**

Tiger (whistle)
With feet

Value:...$5-$10

Tiger, whistle. **$5-$10**

Tinkerbell
Late 1960s, no feet

Value:.......................$200-$250

Tinkerbell. **$200-$250**

Tom

Early 1980s, No feet and with feet
The feline portion of MGM's famous cat and mouse pair. Not released in the U.S. Several versions have been produced.

No feet: ....$25-$35
With feet:..$3-$8
Multi-piece face: ....$5-$10

Tom, no feet (L) **$25-$35**, and with feet **$3-$8**.

Tom, with feet (L & C) **$3-$8**, and multi-piece face (R) **$5-$10**.

Trucks (Rigs)

2005

Trucks can be found in four different cab styles and several different color combinations.

Value: ....$1-$2

Trucks. **$1-$2**
(KP Photo)

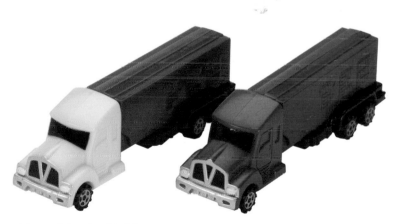

Additional Trucks. **$1-$2**
(KP Photo)

Tuffy

Early 1990s, with feet
A non-U.S. release, Tuffy looks very similar to Jerry,
but has gray face instead of brown.

Painted face:..$3-$5
Multi-piece face: ....$10-$15
Current: ....$2-$4

Tuffy, painted face. **$10-$15**

Tuffy, multi-piece face (L) **$3-$5**, and current **$2-$4**.

Tweenies

2002, with feet
Released in Europe summer of 2002.

Value: .... **$2-$4 each**

Tweenies, Jake and Fizz. **$2-$4**

Tweenies, (L to R) Milo, Bella, and Doodles. **$2-$4**

Tweety

Late 1970s to current, no feet and with feet
The oldest version is hardest to find; it has separate pieces for the eyes (known as removable eyes).

Removable eyes, no feet: ....$20-$25
Painted eyes, no feet: ....$15-$20
Painted eyes, with feet: ....$3-$5
Current: ....$1-$2

Tweety, removable eyes. **$20-$25**

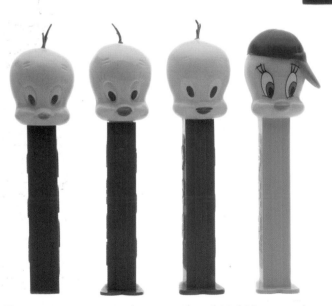

Tweety, (L to R) painted eyes no feet **$15-$20**, painted eyes with feet **$3-$5**, and current version **$1-$2**.

Tyke

Early 1980s, no feet and with feet
Non-U.S. release.

Small painted eyes:..$25-$35
Decal eyes:...$15-$20

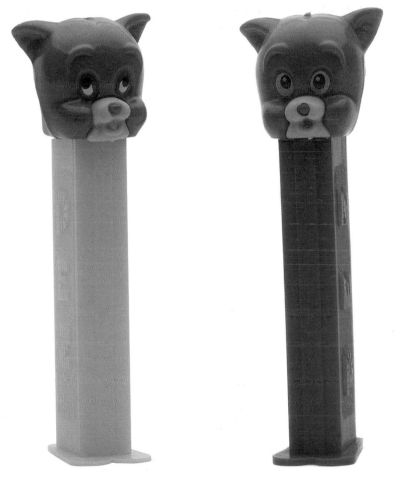

Tyke, small painted eyes. **$25-$35**   Tyke, decal eyes. **$15-$20**

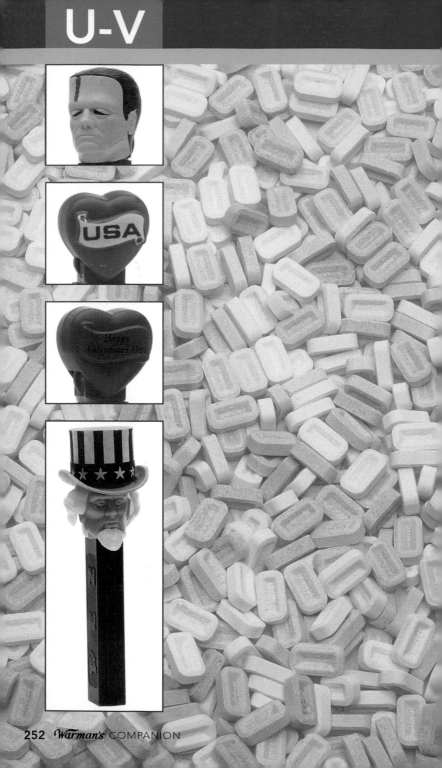

Uncle Sam

Mid-1970s, no feet
Light skin version or tan "club med" version.

Value: ....$175-$200

Uncle Sam. **$175-$200**

Universal Studios Monsters

Mid-1960s, no feet

A highly coveted series among PEZ® collectors and Universal Studio fans. The Creature has a very unique pearlescent stem.

Creature from the Black Lagoon: ....$300-$350
Wolfman: ....$275-$325
Frankenstein: ....$275-$325

Universal Studios Monsters, Wolfman.
$275-$325

Universal Studios Monsters, Creature from the Black Lagoon **$300-$350**, and Frankenstein **$275-$325**.

USA Hearts

2002 mail-in offer. A set of six was offered for $8.95.

Value: ....$1-$2

USA Hearts. **$1-$2**

Valentine

1970s to current, no feet and with feet

Boy and Girl PEZ® Pals on die-cut Valentine cards, no feet, 1970s:................................. $150-$200 each
Boy and Girl PEZ® Pals on Valentine cards, with feet, late 1980s/early 1990s: .... $15-$20 each
Valentine hearts, red stem, no feet:...$1-$3
Valentine hearts, unusual pink stem, no feet: ....$125-$150

Cuddle Cubs 2007: New for Valentines 2007. **$3-$4**
(KP Photo)

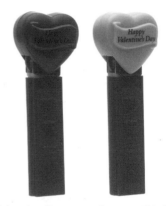

Valentine hearts, red stems. **$1-$3**

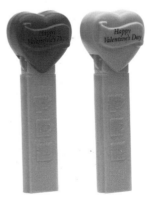

Valentine hearts, unusual pink stem variations. **$125-$150**

Boy and Girl on die-cut Valentine cards from the 1970s.

Boy and Girl on Valentine cards from the 1980s-early 1990s.

Valentine hearts 2005: Versions can be found in purple, red, and hot pink with stenciled stems. 2006 versions have white stems with red and pink stenciled hearts. Both versions can be found with 13 different sayings on the heart. **$1-$2 ea**
(KP Photo)

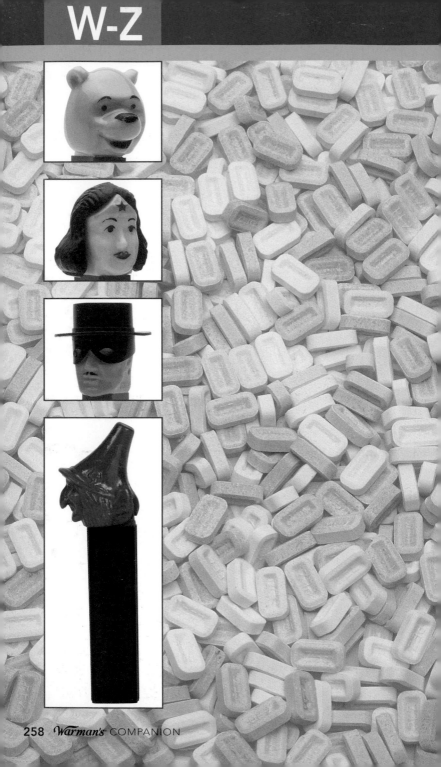

Walgreens Trucks

2005

Sold exclusively by Walgreens drugstores with two different cab styles.

Value: ....**$2-$3**

Walgreens Trucks. **$2-$3**
(KP Photo)

Walmart Rigs

2006-2007

Appearing with four different cab styles, 300,000 of these trucks were produced in 2006 with the famous Walmart logo on the trailer.

Value: ....**$1-$2**

Walmart Rigs 2006. **$1-$2**
(KP Photo)

Walmart trucks 2007: Possible new variations to the successful 2006 offering. **$1-$2**
(KP Photo)

Wile E. Coyote

Early 1980s, no feet and with feet

No feet: .... $45-$65
With feet:.. $35-$45

Wile E. Coyote, with feet. **$35-$45**

Winnie the Pooh

Late 1970s, no feet and with feet
This dispenser was initially released only in Europe. Winnie the Pooh has been quite popular among collectors in general, causing his price to more than double the last few years. Remade and re-released in the summer of 2001, Winnie the Pooh and friends can now be found in the U.S.

No feet: .... $75-$100
With feet:.. $65-$85
Remakes: .... $1-$3

1970s Winnie the Pooh, with feet. **$65-$85**

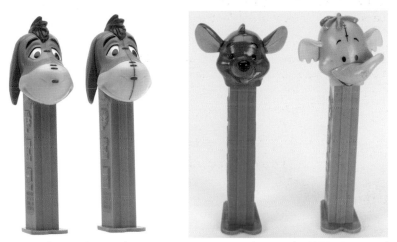

Winnie the Pooh remakes, Eeyore, the version on the right with the line down his nose is the first version and is harder to find. **$1-$3**

Winnie the Pooh 2005: Roo and Lumpy the Heffalump. **$1-$2**
(KP Photo)

Winnie the Pooh remakes, Pooh, Piglet, and Tigger. **$1-$3**

Witch

Late 1950s to current, no feet and with feet

Witch A, orange head, no feet, 1950s: ....$200-$250
Witch B, orange head, slightly taller hat than A, no feet: ...... $2000+
Three-piece Witch, no feet, 1970s: ....$20-$30
Three-piece Witch, no feet, unusual
color combinations: ....$100-$150
Three-piece Witch, with feet:...$3-$5
Witch C: ....$1-$2
Witch C, glow in the dark version (current):.............................$1-$2
"Misfit" version (late 1990s): ....$5-$8
"Convention witch": ....$20-$25

Witch, A version. **$200-$250**

Witch, rare B version.
$2000+
(From the Adam Young collection.)

Glow-in–the-dark Witch, convention version. **$20-$25**

More unusual three-piece Witch variations. **$100-$150**
(From the Maryann Kennedy collection.)

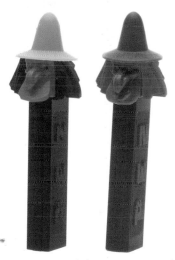

Unusual three-piece Witch variations. **$100-$150**
(From the Johann Patek collection.)

More unusual three-piece Witch variations. **$100-$150**
(From the Maryann Kennedy collection.)

Wolverine

1999, with feet
This is one of the characters from the popular X-Men comic.

Value:..$1-$2

Wolverine. **$1-$2**

Wonder Woman

Late 1970s, no feet and with feet
Two versions of Wonder Woman were produced—
the earlier has a raised star on her headband while
on the second version the star is flat.

Raised star, no feet: ....$20-$25
Raised star, with feet: ....$5-$10
Flat star, with feet (current): ....$1-$2

Wonder Woman, raised star with no feet. **$20-$25**

Unusual Wonder Woman test molds. **$NA**
(From the Johann Patek collection.)

Wonder Woman,
flat star. **$1-$2**

Wounded Soldier

Mid-1970s, no feet

Value: ....$125-$150

Wounded Soldier. **$125-$150**

Yosemite Sam

Mid 1990s, with feet

The shorter mustache on the non-U.S. version allows body parts to be put on the dispenser.

U.S. version:...$1-$2
Non-U.S. version:...$2-$4

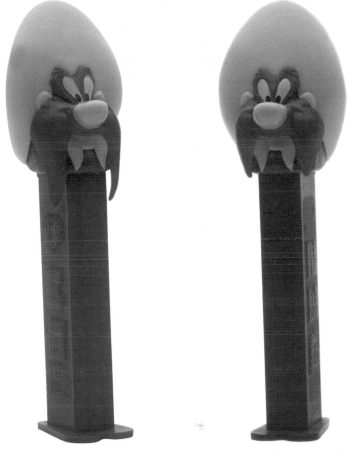

Yosemite Sam, U.S. version. **$1-$2**

Yosemite Sam, non-U.S. version. **$2-$4**

Zorro

1960s, no feet

This dispenser can be found in several different versions: small and large logo and variations of the hat and mask. Some versions have a curved mask and others have a straight mask.

Versions with logo: .... **$100-$125**
Non-logo:.................................. **$75-$100**

Zorro, non-logo. **$75-$100**

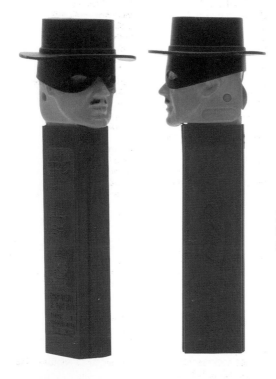

Zorro non-logo (L) **$75-$100**, logo version (R) **$100-$125**.

Index

Index

Identify Your Favorite Icons with Ease!

Warman's® PEZ® Field Guide
Values and Identification
by Shawn Peterson, Edited by Tracy Schmidt

Whether you're a die-hard "Pezhead," a novice collector, or simply a fan of these fantastic and fun candy dispensers, you'll find a lot of details, photos and history in this pocket-sized price guide! Created with you in mind, Warman's® PEZ® Field Guide is the one reference you can truly take with you on every collecting adventure. It easily fits in a purse, backpack, jacket pocket, and even a back pants pocket.

As these beloved candy dispensers continue their reign as popular pop culture collectibles, it's always good to know what you have and its value, as you're scouring shops and shows for new items to add to your collection. From the most collectible dispensers and rare variations, to many recent releases, this "Pezhead" must-have guide delivers the pricing, descriptions and photos you need to accurately identify these icons no matter where you are!

Inside this guide you'll find:
- Hundreds of listings including the most collectible PEZ® dispensers and recent releases
- History of PEZ®
- 400 vibrant color photos that depict true-to-life details

Softcover • 4-3/16 x 5-3/16 • 512 pages
450 color photos
Item# PZFG • $12.99

kp krause publications
An Imprint of F+W Publications

700 East State Street • Iola, WI 54990-0001
715-445-2214 • 888-457-2873
www.krausebooks.com